Table of Contents

INTRODUCTION

Dog Training in our Day and Age

These days, the internet is overflowing with free information on raising puppies and training dogs. Type your question into google or YouTube, and you will be flooded with many colourful training videos, how-to articles and websites. Most of this readily available information is based on positive training methods.

But what exactly is this positive-only method to training puppies and adult dogs? Positive-only basically means that you reward your dog when it does something that you like. For example, you want to teach your puppy how to sit on command. So, once the dog does sit down as it should, you give it a tasty treat. In this way, you teach your dog that sitting down on command gets it something nice. But what to do if your cute new puppy does something naughty, like jumping up at you, or puncturing your hands with its needle-sharp teeth? A positive-only dog trainer would advise you to not correct the unwanted behaviour, but to simply ignore it. Or to try and redirect your puppy's attention. For example, towards sinking its little teeth into a toy, rather than into your hands.

Other approaches to raising puppies and training dogs include terms such as "alpha", "pack leader" and "dominance". And borrowing terminology from the world of wolf packs, where the alpha wolf, or pack leader, is seen behaving quite violently (from our human perspective) towards the less dominant pack members. However, in my experience, these terms sometimes evoke negative associations in people's minds. Such as ruthless dog trainers punishing innocent puppies and making them squeal. Of course, no good dog trainer would apply wanton violence in their work. But yes, there are trainers who apply stronger corrective measures than others.

Embracing a Balanced Approach to Dog Training

Today's community of dog owners seems to strongly gravitate away from those stronger approaches and towards positive reinforcement: Positive-only is widely accepted today as a humane, respectful way of educating our canine companions. However, why are so many owners *still* facing significant problems with their dogs - to the point where they see no other choice but to give up their canine companions? Based on my personal experience, this sad reality is neither the fault of those owners, nor of any specific training method. It is simply a matter of people jumping straight into obedience training when they get their new puppy: Because this is what you do when you get a dog, right? Little do these well-meaning owners know that there is something else they need to do *first*. And this mysterious "something else" is what I call *the missing secret to success*: The foundation of raising perfect canine companions - and of enjoying an amazing, life-long relationship with our dogs.

But before we delve deeper into this missing secret, let's see if we can combine both dog training methods we have mentioned: the positive-only- and the dominance-based approach. Whilst they seem contradictory at first glance, I have seen time and again that elements of both have their place in raising perfect puppies.

When it comes to teaching puppies, reward-based training is an amazing tool, and I personally recommend that we use positive reinforcement at least 95% of the time. Especially in raising puppies, this gentle approach is ideal, as it helps create an ideal atmosphere of learning. Clicker training, a cheerful "YES!", a treat or any other form of immediate praise after a job well done are excellent ways to teach puppies new things. We want them to associate learning with fun, and training sessions should always be something your dog looks forward to.

However, learning can be greatly enhanced if we also implement certain corrective measures. And by that I do NOT mean beating your dog or using any form of violence. Corrective measures can be as gentle as an appropriately timed verbal correction, for example a strong "NO!". Then, after the dog has stopped the unwanted behaviour (for example biting your shoe-laces), you can go straight back to your positive ways. In our example, you could redirect your puppy's attention to a chew toy, and praise it for engaging with that toy.

Taking a balanced approach to puppy-training simply means that you use ALL the different tools in your training toolbox: treats, praise, play - and the occasional correction if needed.

Why are There so many Problem Dogs?

Given what we just said about the benefits of the positive-only method, the way of the "pack leader", and the balanced approach (which in essence combines both), the real question remains:

Why are there still an estimated 670'000 dogs being put down every year in shelters in the US alone?[2]

For example: Why does dog owner Jim Smith[3] from Michigan see no other option than to give up his 12-month-old German Shepherd mix Bello? Jim got Bello when he was a cute little puppy. But after a few months, the already large dog had chewed his kitchen cabinets to pieces, scared off visitors with his (now seriously painful) "puppy-biting" and upset Jim's neighbours with his incessant barking. These neighbours now have called in animal control. Jim tried the positive-only method, but, alas, without success. And now, his promising puppy is facing an untimely death by euthanasia. And why? Because on top of everything else, Bello is lunging at people and trying to bite them when out on a leash. No shelter will take such an "aggressive" dog. Therefore, Jim now sees no other choice than taking Bello to the vet to have him put down.

All the free information on the web about dog training has failed to save Bello from his tragic fate: The life of a perfectly healthy dog, cut short by behavioural problems. And whilst the life of Jim and his family continues, this family now has to overcome the trauma of raising a puppy - only to then have it euthanised. How is Jim going to explain to his children why their best friend is gone forever?

The Missing Secret to Saving Dogs' Lives

More than anything, this book was written to prevent the sad tale of Jim and Bello from repeating itself over and over again - traumatizing entire families in the process. And getting perfectly good dogs killed for something that is not even their fault. Preventing such tragic scenarios from happening is actually quite easy. Provided you know the missing secret to success when it comes to raising perfect puppies - and ultimately, to saving dogs from being put down in shelters all over the world. The one thing that no one really seems to talk about any more: *Leadership*. If you can be your dog's calm, consistent leader, then any form of training is a piece of cake. But if you cannot, then you set yourself and your dog up to fail. Like Jim set Bello up to fail.

In the human world, we value our freedom above everything and we usually do not appreciate being told what to do. But dogs live in a very different world. Contrary to us humans, they absolutely need a calm, consistent canine leader in their lives. A confident person whom they can look to for guidance and direction. We have to give our dogs the structure and boundaries they need to feel safe.

In essence, a dog with a high level canine leader in its life is a happy, well-rounded dog who feels confident, safe and secure. A dog who does not have such a leader in its life will live in fear and anxiety. Now, again, this may seem counter-intuitive, as we associate personal freedom with happiness, but for dogs, it really is the other way round. Were it not, we would live in a world populated by millions of calm and well-behaved dogs, owned by happy, joyful humans.

Instead, we live in a world where millions of dogs get put down because of seemingly irreversible behaviour problems. And in my work as a Canine Behaviourist, I see such problems day in, day out: Countless desperate owners approach me in the hope that I can save their precious puppy from euthanasia. Often, these people come to me after having been turned away by several other trainers. Instead of even trying to help, these "dog-trainers" told them their dog was beyond hope - and they should have it put down. Quite frankly, it breaks my heart to hear these stories. Of course, I do what I can to help those desperate owners and their dogs. And my main reason for writing this book is that I want to reach as many people as possible - *before* they run into serious problems and consider putting an end to their dogs' lives.

Because of my profession, I can personally attest that raising puppies and owning dogs without any structure, boundaries and expectations has proven a recipe for disaster. So, whilst I have personally seen many dogs that are allowed to do whatever they want, I have also seen how many of these dogs are living in fear: Simply because they have no one to give them the guidance they seek, and the direction they desperately need to feel safe. As a result, some of these dogs have developed serious separation anxiety. Others have become dangerously aggressive towards other dogs and humans. And all these undesirable behaviours stem from the complete absence of leadership in these dogs' lives.

LEADERSHIP - the Foundation of Dog Training Success

Let's take a step back for a moment and use an analogy. Say you have bought a plot of land and you want to build a house on it. The home of your dreams. In your mind's eye, you can clearly see the finished house before you - its modern architecture, floor-to-ceiling glass doors, luxury finishes and marble floors. As time passes, the builders finish constructing your dream house. You get the keys, you move in, and you are blissfully happy. But one day, your area is hit by a minor earthquake. And whilst the houses in your neighbourhood only have minor damages, your own beautiful dream home is totally wrecked by the earthquake. Entire sections of the building have collapsed in a pile of rubble, while others now resemble the tower of Pisa. After you have gotten over your first severe shock, you call in the experts. And it turns out that your builders have messed up the foundation layer of your magnificent house. Therefore, it was not able to withstand this minor natural disaster.

Calm, consistent canine leadership is this all-important foundation layer. And your "dream house" is your perfectly trained canine companion - the puppy you have raised with great success. The floor-to-ceiling glass doors, luxury finishes and marble floors are all the amazing things your dog can do: tricks, commands, house manners, behaving well in public and so forth.

Sadly, in my line of work, I see every day how dog owners make exactly the same mistake as the unfortunate house owner in our example: They jump straight into the training aspect of puppy raising. And they just assume that, somehow, the foundation (leadership) will take care of itself. But judging from the thousands of real examples that I have witnessed, I can safely say that this foundation does not take care of itself. It needs to be built with patience and perseverance. And just as there is no getting-rich-quick scheme in business, there is no getting-canine-leadership-quick scheme in the world of dog ownership.

So, once the average puppy owner runs into problems, they jump online and research what to do. Nothing wrong with that. But only a precious few of those online sources inform these dog owners about the basics: About the importance of patiently building that foundation layer of leadership *first*.

From my experience, I can safely say: Without this foundation layer firmly in place, any training you attempt will have little substance to it: There is no real bond connecting you and your dog, because such a deep bond absolutely requires your dog to trust you as its leader. And as a result, the entire construct of your relationship with your dog can fall apart like a house of cards at the first challenge you encounter. Only focusing on the training aspect is like building your house on sand. Unfortunately, that is what everyone seems to be doing.

Your Success is only one Decision Away

So, how can you become a good canine leader who can raise perfect canine companions? Well, this is actually much easier than you might think. Because once you understand the importance of leadership, you are well on your way. Once you make the decision to become a calm, consistent canine leader, your success is only a matter of time. Even if you think you are not cut out to lead anything or anyone: Where there is a will, there is a way, and you will be amazed at how much calm confidence you will gain as a person during this process.

And the main reward for honing your leadership skills is the fulfilling relationship you will enjoy with your dog. A relationship that is marked by excellent communication, by mutual trust and affection. Your own good leadership is the magical key to unlock the treasure trove that is your dog's potential. And this key fits the lock far better than the "key" of purely positive reinforcement.

As a high level canine leader - and really *only* as a high level canine leader - you have a front row seat to one of the most fulfilling experiences life has to offer: The experience of raising and training a perfect puppy, and then seeing that puppy grow into a well-rounded, confident adult dog. Your efforts, your calm consistency and your patience will be rewarded by a perfect canine companion. A dog with whom you share a deep emotional bond. And whom you can easily take on outings, because it will be so well-behaved and obedient. People in public will take notice of this, and appreciate your dog's calm confidence and impeccable manners. No matter what situation occurs, your dog will be able to handle it - thanks to its trust in your guidance.

What this Book can do for You

And it is the dedicated aim of this book to assist you in reaching this goal.

In having this perfect canine companion by your side for the remainder of its natural life. At the same time, in writing this, it is my heartfelt wish for you to enjoy the journey, day by day. To enjoy the colourful, delightful and ever-new experience of raising a puppy - of consciously building a relationship marked by high levels of unshakable trust and mutual affection. Leadership is the basis for all of that. Leadership is your magical key to everything you want to achieve in raising a puppy. And leadership is the missing secret to success.

In this book, I will show you how to become the high-level canine leader you need to be in order to evoke the very best in your puppy. Together, we will discuss various examples of amazing canine leaders and their dogs. And I will reveal to you many real-life stories that I have personally witnessed during my work as a "hands-on" Canine Behaviourist. Illustrated by these true stories and examples, we will dive into the cornerstones of canine leadership - and into easy ways to master them.

Having raised dogs and rehabilitated dogs for nearly 20 years, I have a lot of experience in the field. And I cannot wait to share some of that experience with you, as we embark on this journey together. As you are reading this, I commend you for your eagerness to learn how to raise and train perfect puppies. For your open mind to explore deeper dimensions of dog training that go far beyond the current mainstream-approach. And I am deeply and sincerely honoured by your trust in me and in this book. I am fully committed to making this manual the best tool possible for you to use on your journey. May reading this assist you in becoming your new puppy's high-level canine leader, and in building that solid and trusting relationship that both of you deserve.

Part 1

LEADERSHIP FOR DOG OWNERS

CHAPTER 1

Leadership, Relationship & Communication

Leadership is the foundation for all fruitful dog training. With proper leadership in place, any kind of obedience training or trick training is the proverbial piece of cake. Without that leadership, however, training your dog is far more difficult than it needs to be. And even more importantly: Obedience training will not fix any behavioural problems that might arise in your puppy. If the basis of leadership is missing, then all obedience training is merely a band-aid and not a cure for such problems.

In this first chapter, we are really going to delve into the intricacies of leadership for dog owners. As we begin our journey together, we will discuss why leadership – and everything it entails - is such a huge game changer. Calm, consistent canine leadership is the key component to raising perfect canine companions. Without stress, without headaches, and without the need to spend lots of money on dog trainers. In this first chapter, I will explain why you do not require anything or anyone else. And right now, in this precise moment, you already have everything that you need to succeed in raising the perfect puppy.

In this chapter, I am going to hand you the key to unlock the secret vault of leadership. A vault that is buried – not in other books, courses or programs, but – in yourself. You as a fully established calm consistent canine leader are everything you need, and everything your dog needs, for them to flourish. And for you to enjoy an amazing, fulfilling relationship with your canine best friend. Let's begin!

How Leadership Informs Relationship

Whilst leadership is key, it is intricately connected with relationship and communication. One leads to the other: Imagine a pyramid with leadership as the base, relationship above it and communication at the top level of the pyramid. I like to say that leadership informs relationship, which then informs communication. And you absolutely have to have each level accomplished before you can move on to the next one. So first, let's see how exactly leadership informs relationship.

Diagram Number 1: The Leadership Pyramid

And to better understand the connection between leadership and relationship, we have to ask ourselves:

What exactly do we want from our dogs – and what do THEY want from us?

First and foremost, we want our dogs to be perfect canine companions. And perfect canine companions do not jump up at people, charge out onto busy roads or chase everything that moves. In other words, we do *not* want a dog who makes its own decisions.

Instead, we want a canine companion who looks to us for guidance and direction in all circumstances, scenarios and situations. We want an incorruptible dog who will follow our lead, no matter if we are alone together in the living room or in the middle of Times Square - the most distracting place on the planet - a dog that has enough obedience for us to keep them under control at all times.

THAT is the ESSENCE of being able to have that wonderful canine companion we are looking for.. And that is precisely what I mean when I talk about leadership, about you being that calm consistent leader: An owner whose leadership is respected by their dog at all times. That is what *we* want - and that is *also* what *dogs* want. (The majority of dogs, anyway: Breeds like the Labrador or the Golden Retriever practically come out of the womb ready to embrace us as their leader, with no training whatsoever. These breeds have a deep-rooted, natural desire to seek that guidance and direction from their owners. And because we can get that leadership and relationship so extremely easily from these breeds, they are ideal for first time owners.)

But how does such leadership build an amazing and fulfilling relationship with our dogs? In our pyramid-diagram, we saw the entire base of the pyramid occupied by leadership, and this leadership literally carrying the other two layers (relationship and communication). As we saw, good leadership can be summarized in having a dog who looks up to us for guidance and direction in all circumstances. Which automatically means that the relationship with our dog is based on trust: A dog who looks up to us for guidance and direction will TRUST us to be in control no matter what happens. Such a dog is calm and relaxed, and why? Because it knows that it has nothing to worry about, nothing to be anxious or fearful about. Such a dog knows that they can trust us to take control and to deal with anything that comes our way. Whether that is a dog barking at us on the other side of the road, a person ringing our doorbell or a stranger approaching the dog, wanting to pet it.

Any dog that lives in such a trust-based relationship with their leader, will know that all is well and that they do not have to carry 'the burden of command': Because YOU are the one in charge, they will happily fall in place and leave it to you to make decisions for them. To illustrate what I mean, let's look more closely into the example of a dog barking at you from the other side of the road. So, you are out walking with your dog (let's call him "Max"), minding your own business, and suddenly, another dog (whom we will call "Brutus") aggressively barks at you from across the street.

The other dog is yanking on its leash, lunging and desperately trying to break loose to get to Max. But whilst Brutus' owner is huffing and puffing, evidently struggling to control their raging canine, Max remains calm.

Respecting and trusting your leadership, he knows that he does not have to bark back or lunge at Brutus. Max knows that simply because he has that relationship of trust with you as his leader to fall back on: Even if Max gets a little bit worried by this much larger dog barking, growling and snapping, he has this relationship of trust to fall back on. He knows that you are in charge and that you will *take* charge, should the need to occur. So, all that Max will do, should he get a little bit worried, is, to look up to you for guidance and direction – kind of saying "Uh-oh, that dude over there is kind of big, and he keeps on yelling at me… It's kind of intense, boss, so what do we do?" And your answer would be along the lines of, "Mate, you don't have to worry, we still keep on moving; all I want you to do is walk nicely to heel". In turn, Max would say, "Okay, cool, no worries".

This conversation can either be accompanied by a verbal command, such as "Heel!", or it can be entirely silent. In which case your command to continue walking to heel is being transmitted merely by your example: When Max looks up to you for guidance, he sees that you are not bothered by that other dog. Instead, you keep on moving in the same direction, filled with confidence and assurance. And this is exactly how leadership informs relationship and relationship informs communication: One builds upon the other, and communication is the crowning glory of the pyramid. Having established good leadership leads to a rock-solid relationship which in turn enables you to effortlessly communicate with your dog.

How Relationship Informs Communication

In observing Max's reaction to getting barked at by another dog, we have already jumped ahead a little bit into the realm of communication. And whilst communication is at the top of the pyramid - as it does rely and build upon good leadership and relationship - those three components are not strictly set apart from one another: They interweave as well, a bit like the circles of a Venn diagram. And it is precisely in that middle section of the diagram (the area where all three components) where we want to be with our dogs.

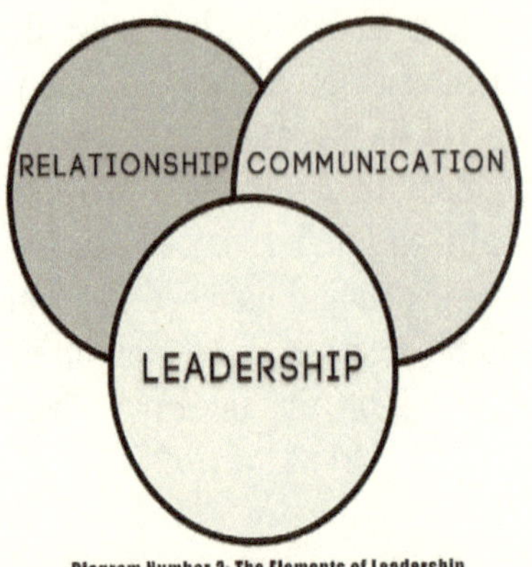

Diagram Number 2: The Elements of Leadership

So, let's say we are a calm consistent leader, and our dog respects that leadership. This then allows us to have that relationship with our dog where it looks to us for guidance and direction, no matter what is happening around us. With leadership firmly in place, relationship and communication then flourish – without it, they are prone to crumble and fail, because their foundation is missing: We cannot get to that point where the dog looks to us for guidance and direction IF they do not trust us as their calm consistent leader.

But how exactly does relationship inform communication? Let's assume that you have established a strong bond with your dog – fantastic. This bond, this close connection provides fertile ground for effortlessly communicating with your dog. And this communication is not just one-way: Once you have built leadership and built that connection, you will be finely tuned into your dog's way of "telling" you things. For example, some owners swear that their dog deliberately informs them about what is going on outside the house by modulating their voice: People strolling by the property will trigger a different kind of bark than a car stopping out front.

In the example of your trusted canine companion "Max", we have already caught a glimpse of what happens if relationship and communication are missing: "Brutus", the large, powerful dog wildly barking at Max from the other side of the road does not have that relationship with his owner. And he certainly does not respect his owner as the leader. In the absence of anyone taking the 'director's chair', Brutus has been left with no other option than to occupy it himself: In his mind, the chair of the leader cannot, *must* not, remain unoccupied. And if his owner will not occupy it, then he himself has to take charge. And decide what is the best way forward in any given situation. So, in the current situation of "strange male dog appearing from around the corner", Brutus decides to attack. But being on a leash, he cannot physically get to Max. So he resorts to start pulling, barking and lunging at the fellow male dog suddenly appearing in his (Brutus') neighbourhood – which means, in his established territory. Quite evidently, Brutus is a dog who has no leadership, no relationship and certainly no communication with its owner.

Now, if Brutus did have a calm consistent leader with whom he enjoyed an excellent relationship, he would not make his own decisions upon spotting Max. Instead, he would look up to his owner for guidance and direction. So, let's say the same situation happens and Brutus goes "Oh wow, there is this weird dog right across the road from us..." , but instead of him thinking, "I need to make a decision on how to respond here", Brutus immediately looks up to his owner for guidance and direction, silently communicating: "Hey boss, how should I respond here?" - Or maybe he does not even ask the question, but simply looks up to see how his boss is dealing with that strange dog appearing. Without a single command being uttered, Brutus quickly comes to the appropriate conclusions: "Ah, he's just moving forward and cracking on, it's not bothering him - that's what I need to do, so I will just move forward and ignore that weird dog, and not let it bother me."

As Brutus is looking up to his owner for guidance, the channel of communication is wide open. Which allows Brutus' owner to respond in whatever way he sees fit: Either by just continuing on, or by giving a "Sit and Stay!" command, for example. But Brutus' owner can also now easily communicate what he does *not* want in that scenario: If Brutus was to growl and get slightly agitated, a short "Leave it!" would cut short any undesired reaction to Max's appearance across the road.

This is where communication happens twofold – or threefold, really: Once we have established leadership and relationship, we can tell our dogs what we DO want and what we DO NOT want. They in turn can communicate to us how they feel about a situation. For example, Brutus' growling could be a signal to his leader that he feels worried by Max's sudden appearance. Which in turn would lead to the owner giving the appropriate guidance. In our example, "Leave it!" signals to Brutus that Max calmly going about his business over there across the street is nothing to get worked up about.

And that is precisely how relationship informs communication, because our dog will look up to us for guidance and direction. They will trust in us, and they will trust in us handling any situation we find ourselves in.

How Communication is used for the Perfect Puppy

So, we have seen how good leadership leads to a solid relationship which then allows clear communication. And now that you have established this amazing connection with your dog – NOW is the time to finally bring in obedience: NOW you have the complete and perfect foundation in place for your success in obedience training. In your case, obedience training your puppy will be easy, stress-free and successful.

Whereas the training efforts of most owners are bound to encounter obstacles and setbacks: As they have jumped directly into obedience, these owners have failed to build the foundation layer first: leadership – relationship – communication. Let's say your neighbour Alice has decided to get a cuddly little Cavapoo puppy for herself and her two young children.

Alice is doing everything by the book: As soon as Susy the puppy moves into their small home, Alice starts house- and crate-training her, and instils basic commands in the little canine: "Sit, "Down', 'Leave it" and so forth. Of course, this is very useful, and as Cavapoos are an intelligent breed, little Susy picks up those commands in no time at all. And after a few weeks, the small fur ball displays an amazing level of obedience, much to Alice's delight. But, alas, whilst Susy performs perfectly in the living room, she gets all agitated when taken for walks in the real world. And after a few months, Susy seems to suffer from a split personality disorder, because she behaves impeccably in the house, but spins out of control as soon as she gets outside.

Susy is now 6 months old and her lack of cooperation when out on a leash is becoming seriously taxing for Alice. This puppy seems to have forgotten every single command she has ever learned. At least, the little Cavapoo is not aggressive to other dogs like our large friend Brutus. But her high-pitched yapping, pulling and spinning as soon as she sees other canines or cats has turned walking her into a chore for her owner. Alice decides to only let Susy off the leash out in the field, as far away from other dogs or cats as possible. But alas, sometimes, Susy covers large distances on her little legs to get to any dog in sight at record speed. She only wants to play, but Alice is afraid that her behaviour might get her bit someday.

Thankfully, Alice and Susy manage to avoid the nightmare-scenario of the adorable fluffy Cavapoo getting bit by a larger dog like Brutus. Instead, one fine summer morning, Alice and Susy run into another dog whilst out walking on that field. Like Brutus, that other dog is very large and could do a lot of damage, if he wanted to. But luckily for our Cavapoo, this dog is extremely well-balanced and well-socialised. He is a yellow Labrador Retriever, his name is Odin, and his owner is Mike, a local farmer.

Both Alice and Mike have their dogs off leash, casually sniffing the ground – at least until they see each other. In that precise moment, two things happen: Susy the Cavapoo starts racing towards Odin as if her life depended upon getting there as fast as possible. Odin, seeing the little tornado sprinting into his direction, pops up his ears, then quickly turns his head and looks toward Mike for guidance and direction. One short pip on Mike's whistle is enough to bring Odin into a nice heel position, where Mike can clip his leash to his collar. Alice, on the other hand, is screaming, yelling and whistling at a dog who completely ignores her. All of her hard work in teaching Susy commands and tricks back home is not helping at all out here in the real world. A world full of distractions, temptations and unpredictable events. Anything can happen out here on the field, or on the streets, whilst you are walking your dog.

So, when these variables and distractions happen (like Odin and Mike coming onto that field), and the dog does not have a strong relationship to its owner, it will most likely 'forget' all the commands that their owner has taught them: a dog without a trusted leader will behave much like Susy, the Cavapoo: Once something unexpected happens on a walk, that dog completely ignores us - instead of looking to us for guidance and direction. Because of this, we have no communication with our dog, to tell them what we want them to do and what not. So instead, that dog acts like a loose cannon, responding in whatever way it sees fit - and *that* is where behavioural problems are prone to occur.

For this reason, you simply cannot have obedience that works in the real world without first having established leadership, which informs relationship - which *then* informs communication. So, when it comes to how communication is used for the perfect puppy – this is exactly how it is used:

No matter what happens in the real world with your dog, you have enough communication established to handle any situation. And you can do this because your dog is looking to you for guidance and direction. This is so incredibly important, because once your dog looks to you for guidance and direction, NOW you have WON. That is it. That is all you need. You have done the hard work; you have laid the foundation for a life-long satisfying and well-balanced connection with your dog.

At that stage, when you are out with your dog and something happens, they will look to you for guidance and direction. All you need to do at this point is to THEN use your basic obedience: "Sit", "Stay", "Come", "Heel" and so forth. If you have got those things, then you have got a perfect dog who is in control in all circumstances and situations - be it in the living room or in Times Square. This is where we can utilize that basic obedience: to keep our dog under control at all times, whatever is going on around us.

Once we have reached this point, people get incredibly envious at the skillset people like Mike have. That morning when she met him and his yellow Lab Odin on the field, Alice would have loved nothing more than to have that same control over her own dog. Now, if Mike wanted to teach Odin the same elaborate obedience-drills and tricks that Alice had taught Susy - doing so would be a proverbial piece of cake: Because of the rock-solid relationship that him and Odin have, training him tricks would be the easiest thing in the world. But people like Mike - and myself, for that matter - are not that interested in trick-training. All we want is to have a dog that we can take with us anywhere in the world. A dog who will look up to us for guidance and direction whenever something unexpected happens. And a dog who will either nicely walk to heel, or who will promptly come and sit next to us when we ask him to, no matter what is going on around us. Such a dog is precisely the perfect canine companion that we want to have.

CHAPTER 2

Lead and Succeed

How to Become a Calm Consistent Canine Leader

So, how exactly do you become a calm consistent canine leader who raises perfect canine companions? The answer is simple: It all boils down to rules, boundaries and expectations – setting those and enforcing them in a calm, consistent manner. That is how you become a canine leader.

When it comes to what exactly these rules, boundaries and expectations are, you can be flexible. For example, some people want their dog on a sofa, and others do not. Personally, I do not mind what your decision is on this, but I do see two caveats. The first one being that you can easily cause confusion and even anxiety in your dog by being inconsistent. So, if you want your dog to be allowed on the sofa, everybody in that household has to be consistent with that rule. Because otherwise you are not being fair to the dog. Inconsistency causes confusion, which then breaks down your leadership and relationship, because then there is no trust. If you are confusing the dog with any inconsistency in leadership, that dog might suddenly find itself in a scary situation: It does not trust that it can look up to you for guidance and direction. CONSISTENCY is so incredibly important, because your dog needs to know that it can ALWAYS look up to you for guidance and direction, no matter what is happening - because you are so robotically consistent with your rules, boundaries and expectations. Now, if you do NOT want the dog on the sofa, it is even more important that everybody in the household sticks to that rule, boundary and expectation.

And the second caveat is that everything good has to come through you (and we will discuss this in much more detail in Chapter 6). So, if you do want your dog to come up on a sofa, that is perfectly fine. But it must be absolutely clear to the dog that this is *your* sofa. The food in your dog's life is your food. The water is your water. Even the toys in your dog's life are your toys. Of course, we want our four-legged companions to have all those wonderful things, and we want them to have the best life in the world. But it must be clear to your dog that it owns nothing, because you are the leader. And in a dog's mind, the leader owns *everything*.

So, in the example of that sofa, it must be crystal-clear to your dog that this alluring piece of furniture entirely belongs to you: Your dog cannot ever make the choice of jumping up on it by itself. If the dog wants to come up to the sofa, first, it must adopt a "Sit and Stay" position and wait for further instruction– calmly, patiently and quietly. It can only jump up once you as the leader give the appropriate command. (Of course, if your dog is still in its puppyhood, you would not allow it to jump up onto any kind of furniture – instead, you would make your puppy "Sit and Stay" for a bit and then lift them up. After you decide it is time for your youngster to leave the sofa again, you would, again, pick them up and put them back on the floor.)

This is an example of how you as a calm consistent leader own and control everything in your dog's life. And of how important it is that your dog receives access to everything in its life - especially everything good - only through you as the leader. As our dogs' leaders, we give them all the good things in their lives, but we also give them rules, boundaries and expectations. We enforce those calmly and consistently, 100% of the time. If we do not think that we can enforce those rules, boundaries and expectations 100% of the time, then we do not ask for them, ever! Otherwise, we are setting our dog up to fail. And we always set our dogs up to succeed. Because trust, relationship and leadership are crucial and they have to be firmly established before we can proceed to anything else.

With dogs, there is no grey area – they are very black and white in their way of functioning, very binary, if you will: With a dog, it is either 1 or 0 - either you are the leader and the sofa (or anything else, for that matter) is yours, or you are not the leader and then the dog is at liberty to challenge you for it. This is why insisting on every good thing in your dog's life being yours is absolutely vital. And this kind of calm consistent leadership will keep your dog on track – simply by reminding it every day that those things belong to the boss. For your dog, this awareness is so immensely important because it actually makes them feel safe and secure. Once you establish leadership by claiming everything as yours, your dog will think: 'This person is the boss, and I am happy with that situation. I know that I can get access to all of those things. All I have to do is sit and wait, be well-mannered, calm and just a wonderful dog, and then I get access to all of those amazing things, like toys, food, cosy sleeping spots, walks and playtimes.'

If a dog is not provided with that kind of consistent leadership, they become insecure, as the burden of having to make every decision for themselves weighs heavily on any dog's shoulders. Such a dog lives in fear and anxiety, because it feels it cannot trust you. Could such a dog verbalise its state of mind, it would say something along the lines of: 'Aaah, I don't know where I'm at with my human - sometimes he reacts like this, sometimes he reacts like that, it's always changing, and it's always different…I don't know what to do, so I'll chew something, because it will make me feel better'

We do not ever want to put our dog into such a state of mind. The sure-fire way to avoid this is simply by maintaining our calm consistent leadership. And that is exactly why, in enforcing rules, boundaries and limitations, we are NEVER sporadic, and we enforce them with calm and poise: We do not scream and shout ,or cry and cringe, we just do it *calmly*, as a good leader would. And we do it *consistently*. That is how we become our dog's calm consistent leader.

Leadership and Breed Selection

As we said before, some dogs breeds like Labradors or Golden Retrievers seem to come out of their mothers' womb as picture-perfect followers. From puppyhood onwards, these dogs are ready and eager to embrace leadership from their owners. And the same applies for most of the other Gundog breeds such as the Flat Coated Retriever, the German Shorthaired Pointer or the Irish Setter. Eager to please their owners, these dogs quite naturally will look to you for guidance and direction. In a similar way, the sheep herding dog breeds are outstanding canine companions who, again, will seek your leadership and actively want to comply with your rules, boundaries and expectations. Examples for such breeds are the German Shepherd, the Belgian Malinois, the Border Collie or the Bearded Collie.

And whilst the canine world provides us with these breeds so delightfully easy to lead, it also harbours the opposite: Breeds which come out of the womb NOT seeking – or needing – leadership. The large, powerful livestock guardian breeds are classic examples for this: Rottweilers, Greater Swiss Mountain Dogs, Turkish Kangals, the Caucasian Shepherds, Estrela Mountain Dogs and their likes. Because of their genetic programming, established over thousands of years, these dogs are born to make decisions for themselves. And that is precisely what we want them to do in a working role: To this day, countless large livestock guardians are on duty all across the globe, defending herds of cattle and flocks of sheep or goats. Working in teams or small groups, these powerful protectors watch over their herd or flock and fight off any predators, such as wolves, coyotes or humans. As the farmers cannot possibly be with the herd up on the mountain or on the pasture 24/7, the dogs will stay and guard the animals. To effectively protect their livestock, these farmers absolutely need those dogs to make their own decisions: Their livelihood depends on it.

However, in this day and age, many people try to raise those independent working dogs for a companion role. Quite often, this goes terribly wrong, people are bitten and those dogs end up being put down. Take the Rottweiler for example, and ask yourself why this breed has such a bad reputation. People buy Rottweiler puppies, thinking they will automatically grow into great guard dogs, whilst being obedient and safe pets. First and foremost, Rottweilers and the other large livestock guardian breeds we mentioned are working dogs, not pets. So, with these strong-willed breeds, the implementation of those rules, boundaries and expectations we talked about becomes even more important. Vital, indeed, as one mistake can result in a dog being put down and even in a person mauled to death: Killed by a dog who has made that decision to attack, without looking to their owner for guidance and direction. What these breeds need more than anything else is having those rules, boundaries and expectations in place, and having them enforced to the T, calmly and consistently, by a good leader.

But not only is enforcing those rules even more important with these livestock guardian breeds – it is also much more difficult than with the majority of other dog breeds. Getting them to understand that they cannot make one single decision for themselves, but have to look to you for guidance and direction, is far harder than with the average Hound, Shepherd Dog or even Terrier. Large livestock guardian breeds (and also some of the more strong-willed guardian and personal protection breeds like the Cane Corso), are *built* to make those decisions for themselves in a working role. So, when we bring them into a companion role where we *need* them to look to us for guidance and direction, they are used to thinking: "Oh, you're giving me a command – but, look, I don't need to do that, because I make the decisions here - if I think there's something wrong, I'll deal with it. So, don't worry if there's another person approaching us, I'll just go and attack them!" And to get those dog breeds to accept that they cannot ever make a decision for themselves is not easy, to say the least. It can be done, but it certainly takes a high level of leadership and a lot of experience.

I am going to delve much more into the vitally important and fascinating topic of breed selection in my second book - and I cannot wait for us to explore this amazing topic together more in depth.

Examples of Great Leadership

So, how does calm, consistent canine leadership look like in the real world? To illustrate my theory about leadership and how to become a good leader, I want to give you some examples that I have witnessed over the years. The people whom I will name here are fellow "dog people" whom I just have a chat with once in a while. They are not clients who need my services as a canine behaviourist. And why? Simply because they are A+ canine leaders who indeed have raised perfect canine companions.

Colonel Jack Davis, Royal Marines, Retired [4]

A few years ago, when Colonel Jack Davis was approaching his retirement age, he started planning out how he was going to spend his time in the future. Being an extremely self-disciplined and structured person, he meticulously wrote down all the new pursuits he wanted to engage in. One of his main priorities was to spend lots of time in the great outdoors. Finally, he would have the time to enjoy hiking and fishing trips whenever he wanted. To accompany him in his endeavours, Jack wanted what he would call "a decent dog" – in other words: A reliable, obedient guard dog whom he could count on to have his back whenever he was out in the middle of nowhere. Jack loves large, powerful guardian breeds, and even though he had never owned a dog before, he went with the Rottweiler. Picking the most confident puppy of the litter, a male, Jack embarked on his new mission: raising "Rambo" into the best possible Rottie.

Fast-forward three years, and Rambo indeed has become an utterly amazing adult dog: Extremely confident and strong-willed, Jack's Rottweiler has a competition-grade level of obedience. He is well-socialised and has impeccable manners, which is why Jack can easily take him everywhere he goes. But most importantly, Rambo's relationship with Jack as his leader is beautiful to witness. Suffice it to say, the retired Colonel has managed to shape his dog into a perfect canine companion. He has become a true ambassador for the breed, showing everyone by example how well-behaved and safe Rottweilers can be.

How exactly did he do that, you might ask, and you would expect that Jack – the novice dog owner – at least hired a trainer or read some books on dog training. Well, I did ask him about this, and, slightly embarrassed, he confessed that he never read a single book on canine education, let alone consulted a trainer. Instead, whilst raising Rambo, he simply employed the same style of leadership that he used in his professional life: He set up clear-cut rules, boundaries and expectations and made sure his "subordinate",

Rambo, understood what exactly they were. Then, he enforced these rules, boundaries and expectations to the letter. Firmly and fairly, Jack continued on, teaching young Rambo basic commands, house manners and the proper way to interact with humans and other dogs.

Of course, Jack had the experience of decades in the Armed Forces to back him up: His self-discipline and his extremely structured approach to handling his responsibilities came in extremely handy when it came to raising Rambo. Being a quite strong-willed and independent dog, even for a Rottweiler, Rambo did test his boundaries once in a while. But Jack was equipped to handle these juvenile outbursts of aggression with calm poise and relentless insistence that Rambo adhere to the rules and boundaries Jack had set up.

Elisabeth O'Neil, Primary School Teacher[5]

Not unlike Jack, Primary School Teacher Elisabeth is quite used to setting and patiently enforcing rules, boundaries and limitations. Again, this skill set has proven its worth back when Elisabeth planned to introduce another pupil into her life: a new puppy, more precisely, a Caucasian Shepherd puppy. Having recently inherited her parents' small farm in the countryside, the School Teacher decided that getting a good guard dog was in order.

Unlike Jack, Elisabeth had owned dogs before when she still lived in the city, but only small breeds. So, for her, moving from a Miniature Pinscher to what is perhaps THE most powerful livestock guardian breed on the planet, was a huge step. Many would even call this a recipe for disaster, and insist that someone was guaranteed to get bit by her bear-like guardian. But Elisabeth stuck to her plan, and bought her puppy from a professional, experienced breeder. After spending lots of time with the litter, she picked a calm and laid-back female whom she names "Nina".

As Nina grew up, Elisabeth consistently employed the principles of good canine leadership without actually knowing it (like Jack, she had never read a book on canine behaviour or training): She set and maintained clear rules, boundaries and expectations with the puppy, not letting Nina get away with anything, and she always insisted that Nina follow her guidance – both in the house and on walks.

A couple of years later, Nina has grown into an impressively massive mature Caucasian Ovcharka who regularly accompanies her when she is out in the fields, riding her horse. If anyone ventures too close to Elisabeth – or the horse – for Nina's comfort, she warns them with her deep, booming barks. And even though Nina does not like to be petted by strangers, she keeps her distance and abstains from attacking people or other dogs.

People like Elisabeth and Jack have raised perfect canine companions simply by being calm, consistent leaders in their professional lives: Their extremely structured approach to everything they do has put them in the ideal position to raise their powerful guardian breed puppies into absolutely amazing adult dogs. But you do not need to have a career in the military or in teaching school children to back you up if you want to raise perfect puppies. In fact, it doesn't even matter whether you have prior leadership experience in any field of your life or not. And in this next section, I will explain why.

The Essence of Leadership

Have you ever wondered why so many dog owners actually look strikingly similar to their four-legged friends? This is such a common phenomenon that various studies have been conducted over the past 15 years to reveal the reasons behind it. Some researchers believe that people subconsciously pick pets that resemble them. In some studies, even outside observers could match persons and pets - based on pictures alone. Scientists have reason to believe that this is a universal phenomenon, as it has been observed in Japan, South America and the United States[6].

But this resemblance between owners and dogs is not confined to outer appearance alone: Oftentimes, owners and dogs also share certain traits such as being insecure, laid-back, outgoing, - or simply calm and confident. So, whilst Jack and Rottie Rambo both are on the calm and confident side of the spectrum, Alice and Susy the Cavapoo from our previous example would be on the opposite end of the scale. And whilst it is quite possible that people pick dogs similar to them in appearance and temperament – at least subconsciously -, I believe there is another reason behind this similarity.

Through many years of hands-on experience working with dogs and educating their owners, I have come to the conclusion that people influence their dogs far more than they think. And by "influence" I do not mean the effort they put into training their dogs, but the *energy*, if you will, that they transmit to them. Simply by being around them. People with a calm, confident and laid-back attitude tend to raise dogs with the same characteristics. And of course, breed-specific attributes play a role in this, as we saw a bit earlier when we talked about leadership and breed selection.

However, I have witnessed many, many cases of the owner's general attitude and strong personality traits actually overriding breed-specific behaviour. For example, the English Greyhound comes with a sky-high prey drive. These lightning-fast sprinters are quite prone to hunt everything in sight. They are also prone to nervous and shy behaviour. And yet, I personally know a farmer who has raised his Greyhound to be a calm, confident and obedient farm-dog who is absolutely trustworthy around chickens, birds, cats, sheep and goats. Recently, this farmer has acquired a Pekinese as a companion dog, and, surprisingly enough, the little one is as calm and obedient as his Greyhound friend. Both have perfect recall off-leash under all kinds of distractions, such as cattle moving around, people coming to the farm etc. Complementing the man on his apparent success in raising such obedient and well-rounded dogs, I asked him what his secret was. He thought about it for a while, then shrugged his shoulders and said: "I don't know – with me, all dogs turn out like that."

The man himself is calm and confident by nature, and his temperament seems to have rubbed off on his canines. Of course, the opposite also applies, and I have come to see many nervous, anxious people turning perfectly good puppies into nervous, anxious and disobedient dogs. Not even by doing anything to the dogs, but simply by being around them, they have influenced their puppies - to the point where they displayed exactly the same characteristics as their owners. Think about it: I am sure you know similar examples yourself. And if not, start observing people and their dogs. As you look deeper into these similarities, you will be amazed at how often people's character is mirrored in their canine companions.

But what does all that mean for you and your ability to be a calm, consistent canine leader who can raise perfect canine companions? Actually, it makes your job even easier, as it gives you yet another tool for your canine leadership toolbox, maybe the most powerful of all: Whilst setting and enforcing rules, boundaries and expectations is supremely important, *your way of being is the ESSENCE of leadership*. Call it your character, energy, personality or whatever you like to call it. But you do not need to be born with an aura of calm, consistent leadership around you to successfully raise perfect puppies – you can develop yourself, mould yourself, to become that leader. This does not need to take a long time, either: Set your intention, set your mind and you will get there much faster than you think.

My goal in writing this book is precisely to help you reach this essence of leadership, because applying the tools (like, setting and enforcing those rules, boundaries and expectations) is great. But only when you can fully embody the essence of leadership in yourself will you be your dog's perfect leader. And not only that: You yourself will feel more confident, strong and self-assured. Less anxious, less nervous and far less stressed. This process of raising your perfect puppy can change you on a profound level. And this is really the beauty of the journey. This is what it is about – sharing your life with an amazing puppy and enjoying the process of growth, of learning, that each new day brings you. Nothing would make me happier than for you to achieve this, for you to discover this essence of leadership in yourself, and all the good that it brings. And perhaps, one day, you and your dog will feature on our blog or in one of our videos – as yet another amazing example of a calm, consistent canine leader who has raised a perfect canine companion.

PART 2

UNDERSTANDING PUPPIES

CHAPTER 1

Puppy Psychology

In the first part of this book, we have discussed the vital importance of leadership for successfully raising and training our dogs. We also have seen how the three elements of leadership, relationship and communication build upon each other – and how they are interconnected. And we have seen why your very way of being is the ESSENCE of leadership.

In this second part of "Raising and Training Perfect Puppies", we will take a step back and delve into the fascinating realm inhabited by puppies and their mothers: To better understand our canine companions, we will take a close look into the private and secluded world of canine mothers and their babies. Why is this so important? In my personal opinion, this is an important step on our journey of raising perfect canine companions: I firmly believe that, in order to understand anything or anyone, we need to know their origins. When it comes to people, we want to know their personal history - which is why Biographies and Autobiographies are so popular. If we are fascinated with a popular Actor, Musician or Athlete, we want to know everything about them. We want answers to questions like: Where are they from? Where did they grow up and in which circumstances? Which events have shaped them into the person they are today? And so forth.

The world of literature is another example for our innate desire to know everything about whomever or whatever fascinates us. Take an avid student of Literature for example: No one keen about understanding the works of William Shakespeare will get around looking into the man's cultural, historical and biographical background. What he wrote as a poet is closely linked to who he was as a person. And to the context of the time, the society and the family into which he was born. This approach makes sense to most people, as they understand that a poet's work is the result of their personality and the conditions around them.

Take Shakespeare's famous play 'The Tragedy of Hamlet, Prince of Denmark'. For more than 400 years, Anglicists have laboured to interpret the story of the young Prince. In their attempts to better understand the piece, they have not left a single stone unturned. And for them, it goes without saying that historical and biographical approaches are necessary to grasp the depths of Shakespeare's play.

But when it comes to interpreting the behaviour of dogs, we tend to follow our gut feeling – completely ignoring this all-important "historical and biographical approach". In other words, we do not take our dog's personal history into consideration. Or their breed, and that breed's original purpose. We do not ask ourselves, "Where is my puppy coming from?", "Who are its parents?", "What temperament does its mother have?", "How has it been socialised by the breeder?" and so forth.

Just like in the world of literature, we cannot possibly know everything – especially if we adopt our puppy from a shelter and do not know who its parents are, or where it started life. But we CAN familiarise ourselves with the different developmental stages that all puppies go through. And, even more importantly, we can learn about the developmental stages that our puppy is going through whilst living with us. Having this information and insight is worth gold, because it gives us a head start in understanding our dogs. Knowledge is power, and when it comes to raising puppies into perfect canine companions, we need all the power we can get!

Setting your Puppy up for Success

In Part 1 of this book, we have touched upon rules, boundaries and expectations – using your trusted sofa as an example - and stating how vitally important it is that you be consistent in calmly enforcing those rules, boundaries and expectations. In this chapter, we are going to focus on the expectations' piece of the puzzle: My dedicated aim for Part 2 is to give you realistic expectations about your puppy.

In this way, you are setting yourself and your puppy up to win. Why? Because you know beforehand what to expect at which age. Let's say that your puppy is 6 months old right now. You know that a second fear phase is right around the corner, as well as a second chewing phase, as now your pup's adult teeth have fully developed. Prepared in this way, you have the power to proactively manage your puppy's needs. For example, you can prevent chewing on your shoes by getting your dog a few more durable chew toys. And when your pup suddenly seems spooked by lots of things at once, you are prepared. In this way, you can calmly and consistently lead your dog through these experiences.

THIS is how you succeed: Knowing these things gives you the power to address them in the best way possible – for yourself, your puppy and everyone else involved.

Pitfalls in Puppy Psychology

This chapter has been written to provide you with an overview of the developmental cycles of young dogs – starting from the time they are born, and all the way up to the age of 18 months (which marks the transition from adolescence to adulthood for most breeds). This information will provide you with realistic expectations: You will know what is going to happen in your puppy's mind and body before it happens. In this way, you can successfully tackle even the most feared stages in puppy development, like the chewing phase and the "rebel stage" of canine adolescence.

This information will give you empathy for your dog, and will empower you to raise them with ease and joy. Because, contrary to most puppy owners, you will know exactly what you can expect from your puppy at any given age: what you can ask of them - and what would be too much for them. After reading this chapter, you will have another powerful tool in your puppy-raising toolbox: The knowledge of a puppy's very specific needs and challenges at any given age.

However, there is a potential pitfall to this knowledge of the developmental stages. And I want you to be aware of this before we fully dive into this fascinating topic. I have witnessed this phenomenon over and over again: People come to me because, for example, they think their puppy is reacting overly fearfully, because it has suddenly started barking at motorcycles. When I ask how old the dog is, it turns out it is around the 7 month mark – so, as we mentioned before, smack in the middle of the second fear phase that puppies go through on their journey to adulthood. Of course, I tell them this, and I reassure them, saying how completely normal it is for a puppy to behave in this way.

And then, they go back home, thinking something along the lines of, "Ah, my puppy is just going through this fear stage, so I don't need to worry. Will said it's normal for her to bark at those motorcycles, so I guess I just let her do it for now." But this is not at all the take-away I intended – simply because unruly (in this case, reactive) behaviour does not correct itself: Fear stage or not, you cannot afford to ignore failure. Instead, you always need to address such behaviour, correct it and then redirect the dog to behave in more desirable ways. In our example of the motorcycle, this could mean the dog goes into a nice "Sit and Stay" after it has been verbally corrected for barking.

It all goes back to the importance of leadership, rules, boundaries and expectations – you absolutely have to enforce those calmly and consistently, 100% of the time. Remember our example of your sofa and how crucial consistency is for your dog's well-being? This consistency remains key throughout your puppy's life, and right now is the perfect time to begin enforcing your rules, boundaries and expectations. You can, and should, have empathy for what your puppy is going through, in this case the fear of motorbikes. But you still have to insist on those rules - calmly, consistently, and patiently.

In our example of the motorcycle, as your calm, consistent leader-self, you would think to yourself: 'Ah, okay, Will said it's normal that my pup is going through this fear-stage. So, the next time I hear a motorbike approaching, I will ask her to walk to heel. If she starts getting antsy, I will give a short, sharp "Leave it!"-command before she goes too far into a fear-mode. She loves those beef-treats, so I'll redirect her attention with those – leading her to focus away from the motorbike and back towards walking to heel.'

Of course, this is just an example, and we will go into the ins and outs of puppy-training in the following chapters. But ideally, you want to use the information in this chapter in this way: Use it to better understand your puppy's behaviour and to have empathy for the dog. But at the same time, calmly and patiently correct the unwanted behaviour - knowing that not doing so would be setting your dog up to fail.

Finding the Perfect Breeder for your Puppy

This book is dedicated to helping you raise wonderful dogs. One of the prerequisites of raising an amazing canine companion is picking the perfect puppy for you in the first place. Let me explain: If you want to adopt a puppy from a shelter, that is amazing. Personally, I am a great advocate of adopting, simply because it can save a dog's life. But if you have your eyes set on a very specific breed, your local shelter might not have dogs of that breed available – and much less so, puppies. This leaves you with the necessity of choosing a breeder. And finding the right breeder is extremely important: Given the litter is born and initially raised in their facilities, they have the unique opportunity to influence your future puppy during the first two months of its life.

And their role is so important because puppies need proper socialization throughout their lives in order to become well-adjusted adults. By the time you bring your pup home, it should have been socialised with plenty of different people, including children, and friendly adult dogs. Ideally, your dog will have been exposed to many different sounds, like vacuum cleaners, hairdryers, kitchen appliances, cars, and so forth.

And even though there are many amazing hobby-breeders out there who absolutely love their dogs and want only the best for their puppies – personal experience has led me to recommend professional breeders. Simply because young dogs are so extremely impressionable during the first few weeks of their lives. And pro-breeders who know what they are doing will put their litters through a systematic socialisation-schedule. This in itself can make the difference between you receiving a shy puppy who tries to hide in a corner for the first few days, and a happy-go-lucky pup who joyfully engages with everyone in the household.

A reputable, professional breeder is also most likely to abstain from breeding unbalanced dogs. In this way, they prevent overly aggressive or overly fearful dogs from passing those unbalanced traits onto the next generation. This is very important! Take powerful and potentially even lethal breeds like the German Shepherd or the Alapaha Blue Blood Bulldog as examples for this. As aggression is passed on genetically to some degree, there are bloodlines out there that are well-known for their aggressive tendencies.

But you do not have to take your breeder's word for it when it comes to avoiding such unwanted tendencies in your puppy's parents: Simply ask them to let you meet both parents – especially the mother, as she is the one with the most influence over your pup's early development. Take your time meeting and greeting that mother dog. Pet her and closely observe her behaviour, both towards you (the stranger) and towards the breeder (her leader). If she is too aggressive or shy for you to touch her, beware: She easily could influence her puppies to behave in similar ways – not only by passing on her genes to them, but, most importantly, by her example. After all, the mother is her babies' very first leader, their guide and their role model. She not only nurtures them, but she teaches them how to behave around humans and other dogs.

CHAPTER 2

Puppy Developmental Stages (from Birth to 18 Months)

When we hear the word "puppy", we commonly think about a cute and cuddly little dog. But up to which age is a dog a puppy? There is no one-size-fits-all answer to this question, as we have so many different dog breeds on the planet. In general , the age that marks your puppy's transition into adulthood depends on its breed and size. Small breeds reach adulthood between six and eight months, whereas giant breeds can take up to three years to fully mature physically and mentally! Medium breeds reach their adult size around the one year mark, and large breeds take between 14 and 16 months. So, in essence: the bigger the breed, the longer it takes them to grow up.

So, let's get into the "meat" of this chapter and really look into the different developmental stages of our canine companions. And whilst some schools of thought name seven stages, I am going to stick with the five most commonly know ones:

1. Neonatal period (from birth to 2 weeks)
2. Transitional period (2 to 4 weeks)
3. Socialisation period (4 to 12 weeks)
4. Ranking period (3 to 6 months)
5. Adolescence (6 to 18 months)

1. Neonatal Period (from Birth to 2 Weeks)

Puppies enter the world with their eyes and ears closed. However, they can already smell, taste and touch. Instinctively, they seek warmth from their mother and littermates and they need their Mom's stimulation to pass stool and urine. During the neonatal stage, puppies sleep around 90% of the time and spend the majority of their waking life with feeding. Contrary to human babies, puppies come into this world as veritable little learning machines: They already react to the behaviour of their mother and littermates. This is how, even at this tender age, they learn simple, but invaluable social skills. These skills are the foundations for a successful canine life. Mother nature truly wastes no time: Whilst these tiny puppies are crawling on top of each other, aiming for their mother's nipples, they already practise coordination. They are also busy establishing a hierarchy within the litter: Even now, the stronger, more determined pups will push the others aside to secure the best feeding spot.

Newly born puppies appear extremely vulnerable during the first two weeks of their lives, but their brains and bodies are developing with stunning speed: Within only one week, their birth weight actually doubles. Also, their susceptible brains absorb any available information, storing it as reference for the future. For example, if a dog is handled a lot during this time by different people, it learns that humans touching them is a very good thing - and nothing to be afraid of.

This is exactly why expert breeders use the neonatal period wisely: handling their puppies several times a day and exposing them to different sensations (for example the feel of a hair dryer gently blowing on their fur, or the sensation of nail clippers touching their claws). In this way, professional breeders stimulate and accelerate the pup's physical and mental development. Particularly proactive breeders of high-level utility dogs - like working line German Shepherds, Malinois, Labradors or Border Collies -, even go further: They expose their puppies to ENS exercises (short for Early Neurological Stimulation), combined with early scent introduction exercises. In this way, they are giving the dogs an invaluable headstart for their future roles as tracking dogs, search & rescue dogs or drug detection dogs. To better prepare their puppies for future challenges in their lives, such breeders expose them to different objects and textures. For example, they might put a lightweight cardboard tube into the litter box, that moves when the little dogs touch it.

2. Transitional Period (2 to 4 Weeks)

The transitional period is an exciting time for a young puppy, as it finally gets to see the world through its own eyes. During this stage, the little canine will start its first, and adorably clumsy, attempts to walk. Also, now is the time where its baby teeth are coming in. Its sense of smell and hearing develops, and the pup learns to operate its little tail to perform wagging-moves. So, within four short weeks, you already have a young dog who can stand up, walk, wag its tail, eliminate without needing stimulation - and even bark!

During the transitional period, good breeders will continue handling the puppies. But now that all of their senses are active, the young dogs can experience sights and sounds for the first time ever. This is a perfect opportunity for breeders to introduce them to many different sights and sounds, such as different people and animals, household machines, squeaky toys and so forth. Acquainting puppies with human voices and the different noises they are likely to experience in their new home is very important: What puppies learn in this early transition period has the power to greatly facilitate their transition into their owner's household. Knowing this, expert breeders routinely introduce new background voices, noises and environmental sights to the young dogs. As they know no fear at this stage of their development, puppies can be quite easily desensitized to loud noises, such as screaming kids, honking cars or fireworks. (If none of those are readily available at the breeder's house, playing a youtube video containing those sounds is the next best thing.)

3. Socialisation Period (4 to 12 Weeks)

In the course of the socialisation period, puppies begin to grow rapidly - even to the point where they seem bigger in the morning than they were the night before: Most of the growth happens whilst the young dogs are sleeping. During this extremely important developmental stage, puppies learn how to coordinate their movements. Together with their littermates, they start exploring their environment, smelling everything, playing with each other and becoming quite active in general.

During this stage - usually around the 5th or 6th week -, potential buyers can visit the litter to select their new canine companion. Which is why this juvenile developmental stage preceding puberty is crucial for your puppy, as well as for yourself: Whilst young dogs are very curious and inquisitive in general, some of them will be more investigative than others. This is normal, but at the same time, the puppies' behaviour towards each other and towards you as a visitor gives you valuable clues about their personality and energy levels. Which, of course, will continue to develop throughout the young dog's puppyhood and adolescence. However, the core temperament more or less will stay the same for the rest of the dog's life.

Around this time, the puppies will have developed sufficiently for you to evaluate their temperament. If you can get the privilege to be the first person to select from the litter, I would highly recommend doing so. (Some breeders operate on a first come, first serve basis, whilst others ask for a certain amount of money for pick of the litter privileges.) I can say from personal experience that temperament selection plays a huge, massive role in picking the perfect puppy. In some cases, it even trumps breed selection. Why?

Let me give you an example of an overwhelmed novice dog owner who recently wrote to me about his new Pomeranian puppy. The man had picked this breed because he wanted a sweet, gentle and cuddly companion dog. What he got instead was a fluffy whirlwind of a puppy: an over-excited, hyper-energetic little canine, unable to sit still for one single minute - let alone focus on any commands he tried to instill in it.

To say that puppy training was a challenge for that owner would be an epic understatement. In all likelihood, this man had picked the most outgoing and curious puppy of the litter, no doubt charmed by an adorable little fur ball being so very excited to meet him. Had he taken a medium-energy puppy instead - not the shyest one, but a more relaxed, laid-back animal - his life would no doubt have been easier.

As the socialisation period is so incredibly important for a dog's development, breeders will proactively introduce their litters to even more different people, as well as friendly and fully vaccinated dogs. Around five weeks after their birth, puppies are already quite aware of their environment - and curious about it. Getting more active in playing and exploring their surroundings, they are open to embrace the fascinating world "out there", that is full of exciting scents, sights and sounds.

Now is also the perfect time for breeders to provide the puppies with as many positive experiences around humans as possible: Any good experience with people that occurs in the fifths, sixths, and sevenths week of age has a large impact on the dog's future way of interacting. When the puppies are 6 to 7 weeks old, an excellent breeder will start training them to walk on a leash for very short periods of time. Ideally, they will also teach the puppies to go into a crate on command as well as to carry out simple commands, like "Come", "Sit" and "Down".

The Perfect Time to Bring your Puppy Home

Even though puppies start moving around and interacting quite a bit from the 5th week onwards, they should not be moving into their future homes until around the 8 week mark. A puppy being decently mobile and supplementing its mother's milk with solid food around 5 weeks of age is not out of the usual. However, this should never be a signal for breeders to start giving their puppies out to future owners. Of course, any reputable breeder will know this and not permit you to pick up your puppy until they are 8 weeks old.

The reasons for this are two-fold: Firstly, young dogs absolutely need their mother's milk for nutrition, and secondly, they need to learn vital life lessons from the mother and littermates during the period between weeks 5 and 8. This is the time when pups learn the ins and outs of canine communication as well as inhibited play biting. Which is especially important for their successful integration into a human household: Many owners complain that their puppies are behaving like piranhas, shamelessly biting down hard on human hands and feet with their razor-sharp little puppy teeth. These play-attacks may seem cute for a bit. But before too long, you will just want your puppy to stop, especially as they are growing so fast, increasing their bite-power in the process. However, if your dog has not learned bite-inhibition from its Mom and littermates, it has no way of knowing how much pressure is too much. Or why it should stop play-biting humans altogether. Many cases of aggressive behaviour can be traced back to a puppy who has been taken away from its mother too soon – usually at just 6 or barely 7 weeks of age.

Once the puppy you have chosen from the litter is 8 weeks old and you visit the breeder a second time, this is it: Your journey together has officially started. At this age, your puppy is already fairly mobile, used to eating solid food and able to learn simple commands like "Sit" and "Come". Of course, you want to start on house-training the new family member right away.

After you have bonded with your new puppy and introduced them into the Do's and Don'ts of your household, be prepared to help them through the first "fear" period. This phase lasts roughly from week 8 to week 10, and is marked by your pup getting spooked easily – and by pretty much anything: The triggers for this fear differ from dog to dog, but the best way to help them through this experience is by calm, consistent leadership, and lots of patience: Follow through on the rules, boundaries and expectations that you have set for your dog, reward them whenever they comply – but never ever reward them for being fearful!

This is the biggest mistake people make. Instead, when you notice your puppy is spiralling into a fear-space, re-focus their attention to a voice command. Then reward the positive behaviour, but do not give in to the temptation to comfort and coddle your puppy.

Between weeks 8 and 12 is the perfect time to instill voice commands and manners into your puppy, as they will pay close attention to you, always in an attempt to figure out where they belong in this new situation of living with humans. For the same reason, this stage is invaluable when it comes to socialising the dog: Its natural tendency in this phase is to hone its social skills. I cannot emphasise enough how important it is that you use this window of opportunity wisely – and introduce your puppy to as many friendly people and dogs as possible. Of course, as your puppy has not received all of its shots yet at that time, you want to be very cautious with this. I recommend you speak with your vet about this even before you bring your puppy home.

Personally, I always take full advantage of this socialisation period between the 8th and the 12th week. For example, I take all the puppies I raise to the homes of friends and family - and I invite people over to my house to engage with the puppy. Also, I take them with me in the car and carry them around shopping centres, coffee shops and other places that allow dogs in. In this way, I ensure that, by the time they are 3 months old, my puppies have been exposed to as many different positive situations as possible.

4. Ranking Period (3 to 6 Months)

The Socialisation Period is followed by the so-called Ranking Period. During this developmental stage, your puppy is extremely susceptible to the influence of its playmates, be it humans or other dogs. In these three months, your youngster will use canine body-language (such as posturing, mounting and rolling over) to establish its hierarchical position in the family. Whilst playfully assuming dominant and submissive positions, your dog will also play-bite its "sparring partners".

The ranking period is a prime time for chewing – as well as chewing issues -, as your puppy's milk teeth are replaced by its adult teeth between 4 and 6 months. And to make things more interesting, they go through a second fear stage during this time. But as you are already experienced in handling this, it will be easier to manage this time round. Just remember to stay calm, consistent and patient in leading your dog through this second fear phase.

During this pre-adolescent period between 4 and 6 months, you also will notice a gradual increase in your puppy's curiosity, confidence and independence: The young dog will explore its environment more and more, leaving your side to venture into the "great unknown". Of course, this increase in independence and zest for exploration might make training more difficult. But the good news is that your puppy's attention span now allows it to learn commands quicker than before. Also, your youngster now has more "staying power", which means you can extend the time you want them to stay put in a Sit- or Down-position. Just remain calm, consistent and patient during training sessions. Incorporate distractions (like background noises, nearby traffic etc.) slowly and gradually. This period is crucial to establishing and cementing a strong enough bond with your puppy for them to respect your leadership. Because watch out - the trials and tribulations of adolescence are about to hit both of you square on around the 6 months mark.

5. Adolescence (6 to 18 Months)
Physiological Changes

Canine adolescence begins at roughly the age of 6 months. Again, this age can vary depending on the dog's size and breed. Also, just because your dog is 18 months old, this does not mean that they are done growing - unless you have a very small breed. Whilst your large or giant pup will "officially" be a dog after the adolescence stage, they will continue to fill out: They might stop growing larger at the wither, but will still gain muscle over time. Also, their bones will continue to grow stronger, especially the head. Take giant breeds of the Mastiff-type, for example, such as the Cane Corso, the Presa Canario, the Great Pyrenees or the Caucasian Shepherd. The big, blocky heads of those big boys - and girls -, develop until roughly 3 years of age. And their psychological development is aligned to this slow pace of maturing. Which of course surprises many owners, as they think their dog is done with being an adolescent, just because it has reached the 18 months mark. Little did they know that nature had gifted them with 6 months more of canine teenage-behaviour!

As we said before: When it comes to your puppy entering into adulthood, the rule of thumb is that smaller-sized dogs get there quicker, and the larger the dog, the longer it takes. Also, the growth of mixed breed puppies may differ from purebred ones.

On a physiological level, what happens during adolescence is that growth will slowly come to an end and your puppy's soft and fluffy baby fur is being replaced by a corser adult coat. Also, just like humans, dogs mature sexually during their teenage period: Females usually begin to go into heat between 6 and 12 months of age (the smaller the dog, the earlier the first cycle will occur). Males will start to develop an interest in the other gender that is far less platonic than it was during the stage of innocent puppyhood.

In addition, they will start to mark their territory. In other words, they begin lifting their hind legs to ensure that their precious scent gets onto as many prominent places as possible: trees, hydrants, fence posts and so forth. Humping other dogs and even humans is another typical behaviour for adolescent male canines (unless they have already been neutered at this young age). As your puppy's adult teeth will usually have fully developed around the 6 months mark, be prepared for the second chewing stage that lasts up to around 9 months.

Behavioural Changes

Canine adolescents come with a veritable bouquet of challenges - both for your puppy and for yourself. But knowing what to expect and at which age, you will be equipped in the best way possible. As a calm, consistent canine leader, you will know how to deal with inappropriate teenage behaviors. Simply by enforcing your rules, boundaries and limitations - 100% of the time, calmly and patiently- , you will persevere. And before you know it, your puppy will emerge on the other end of that long and sometimes scary tunnel that is canine adolescence.

By the time your dog enters into the equivalent of the human teenage years, it will see the world around it more like an adult dog would: Gone are the days where your puppy rarely leaves your side on a walk off-leash. Now, it is quite easy for them to get tempted into following scents, sights and sounds that they deem more interesting than you. Such as the trails of rabbits, foxes and deer in the forest, a cat appearing out of nowhere or the sound of other dogs barking behind a fence. During the trials of the teenage period, your dog will be less responsive to your calls - even if you had established an amazing recall before. And when your dog does finally come back to you, instead of sitting down in a nice heel position like it used to, it may bark at you, run around in circles or display other behaviour typical for playtimes. All this is part of the journey. It is simply one of the many different ways your puppy may devise to test the boundaries and expectations you have put in place. And whatever your puppy may do, it is vital that you maintain them.

If in Doubt, Return to the Basics

But whilst the vast majority of puppy owners reel under the impact of the adolescence phase, you will come prepared! Equipped with a toolbox full of different strategies, you and your dog will get through this together, as a team. Rather than getting stressed-out from your "teenager's" antics, you will persevere - calmly enforcing those all-important rules, boundaries and limitations to the T. With no if's and but's. And for you, there is no reason in the world to get stressed-out or to lose your balance: Why would you, given that you are in full control of every situation that could possibly occur at all times? Raising puppies can be a daunting task - no doubt about that - , but it is not rocket science. You can absolutely master this challenge, and enjoy every single step of the process.

Should you struggle with impatience at any point, simply take a deep breath, relax, and return to the basics: Good leadership is the basis for everything - it leads to a good relationship with your dog, which in turn greatly facilitates communication. How do you become a good leader? Simply by setting rules, boundaries and limitations, and then enforcing them in a calm and consistent manner, as any good leader would.

In essence, this is all you need to know to master the trials and tribulations of canine adolescence. And if you are really starting to lose your nerve and you cannot see how you can possibly put up with such a stubborn, uncooperative young dog, simply focus on leadership. Tune in with the feeling of being in charge, of being an amazing canine leader. If you want, say to yourself: "I am a calm, consistent canine leader." Repeat that like a mantra, until you feel calmer. Also, reinforce the leadership vibe with body posture: Sit, stand and walk in an upright position, chest out, eyes forward, feeling sure of yourself - and proud of yourself. And you should be! In this world full of trouble and conflict, anyone with the calm and collected countenance of a leader counts. With this, you contribute positively to the well-being of your dog, your family members, your friends and even your neighbours. But you yourself will reap the highest reward possible: You are going to feel so much better about yourself after you have practised this attitude for a while. The attitude of a winner, of a competent leader who knows what they are doing.

Even if you are presently filled with self-doubt, anxiety or distrust about this concept of leadership, you still can absolutely be a perfect canine leader. Again, raising and training dogs is not rocket science, and neither do you need diplomas or testimonials for it. As a calm, consistent canine leader, you are a person who is sure of themselves, who knows what they are doing - and who is the undisputed master of every situation or circumstance that might arise. Not only whilst in the company of their dogs, but also in every other aspect of their lives.

PART 3

CORE PRINCIPLES OF PUPPY TRAINING

Now that we have covered the developmental stages that every puppy moves through on its journey to adulthood, it is time to really get into the core principles of puppy training: The How-To of raising puppies into perfect canine companions. And in this third part of our book, we are going to delve into the principles of successfully molding puppies into wonderful calm, obedient and well-mannered dogs.

Here, we will look at the three pillars of puppy training. We will see how they relate to the three key elements that we have discussed before: leadership, relationship and communication. The information in this chapter is designed to give you a perfect understanding of how to reach the ultimate goal of puppy training. Which is having this wonderful, dependable dog whom you can take with you everywhere. So, let's jump straight into these fascinating topics – and we begin with the basics of puppy training.

CHAPTER 1

Manners - Socialization - Obedience

The Core Principles of Puppy Training

Socialization, manners and obedience are the three basic principles of puppy training. In our diagram below, we see the Pyramid structure we discussed before, depicting leadership, relationship and communication - and how they build upon each other. But now, we have three additional elements sitting in a circle on top of that pyramid: manners, socialization and obedience. These are the CORE TRAINING REQUIREMENTS for raising perfect puppies.

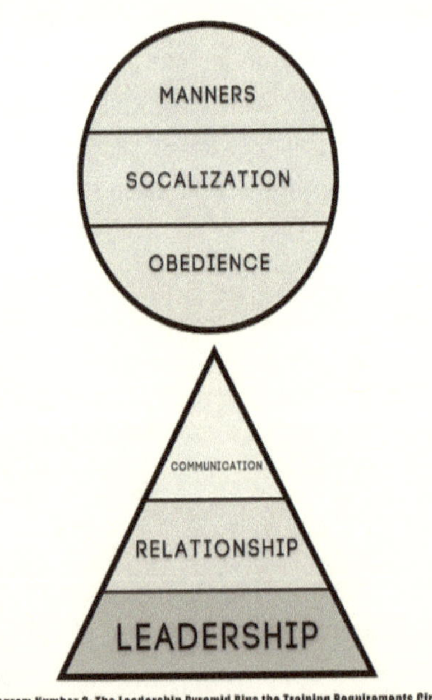

Diagram Number 3: The Leadership Pyramid Plus the Training Requirements Circle

Let me explain what I mean by that, because these three core training requirements are no less important than the foundation layers of leadership, relationship and communication. So, let's assume we have done everything right so far with our young dog: We have established calm consistent leadership, and we have built that trusting, beautiful relationship that we want to have with our dogs. And as a result, we can now - and only now! - effectively communicate with our dogs.

There is a natural crossover between the triad of manners, socialization and obedience. And yet, when it comes to emphasising one above the others, I personally put teaching manners and socialization slightly ahead of obedience. Let me explain why that is: As we have seen before, too many well-meaning owners focus only on obedience, completely disregarding the importance of leadership and relationship. The very same applies to the core training requirements: By and large, people are unaware of the crucial importance of teaching their puppies good manners. And of socializing them from an early age onwards. Instead, they jump straight into obedience and start teaching their puppy basic commands.

Not that there's anything wrong with that - and we will absolutely discuss teaching commands in this book. Then, once you have successfully taught your dog the basic commands, you can take obedience training as far as you want to, even up to competition levels. But, contrary to the vast majority of dog owners, *you* will have a rock-solid foundation to build upon.

So, obedience is necessary. But after working with dogs and their owners for more than two decades, I am firmly convinced that you cannot leave manners and socialization out of the equation - and expect to have a well-rounded dog. And just as obedience alone bears little fruit without leadership, relationship and communication, the same applies here: Obedience needs to be complemented with socialization and manners.

Now, let's talk about the second training requirement, which is socialization. In our previous chapter, we have already seen the vital importance of socialization when we discussed the different development stages of puppies: These stages close at certain times in a dog's life, and after that, we will have missed the chance to socialise them with ease. So, in essence, nature is giving us certain windows of opportunity with these different developmental phases that are designed for socializing a young dog. And once these windows close, our work will be much harder. Of course, the main reason why socialization is so very important is that it allows the dog to be calm and relaxed in any given situation. Which then makes it much easier for that dog to look to you for guidance and direction. So that is where socialization fits into the puzzle.

Now, the third training requirement is manners, which is every bit as important as socialization and obedience. Again, all three aspects are needed to "come full circle" with training our puppies, and they are closely interconnected. Take the command "Sit & Stay" for example. This is one of the most useful commands you will ever teach your dog. And it is invaluable when it comes to teaching manners. Because once you have this command firmly established, you can easily utilize it in a wide variety of different situations. Let's take the scenario of you coming home from work as an example. Whilst most dog owners will be greeted by an overly excited canine who jumps on them and around them as soon as they walk in the door, *your* experience will be very different. Of course, your dog will be excited to see you. But also, he has learned how to greet people properly and politely: Your dog knows that he must offer a well-mannered Sit & Stay before receiving any praise or attention.

Or let's take the example of preparing your dog's dinner. Again, most dogs will be barking, jumping and yelping as soon as they see their owners pick up the food bowl. Not yours however – your canine companion will sit and stay, quietly allowing you to put the food down and then wait until you tell them that they can have access to that food. Another example is play: We do not want a dog who decides what we have to do, and when. Again, most people's dogs will start yelping, barking, nipping and dropping toys on their laps when they want to play. YOUR canine companion, however, is going to be well-mannered, patient and quiet, waiting for you to initiate play sessions - if and when you see fit.

All these examples illustrate just how incredibly important impeccable manners are. And I fully believe that having an amazing canine companion stems from manners much more than it does from obedience. Personally, I would much rather have a well-socialized, well-mannered dog than a well-socialized, obedient dog with poor manners. But of course, for any dog to be a truly perfect canine companion, all three boxes must be ticked, so to speak: Such a dog has to be well-socialized, well-mannered *and* obedient.

Coming Full Circle - the Pinnacle of Puppy Training

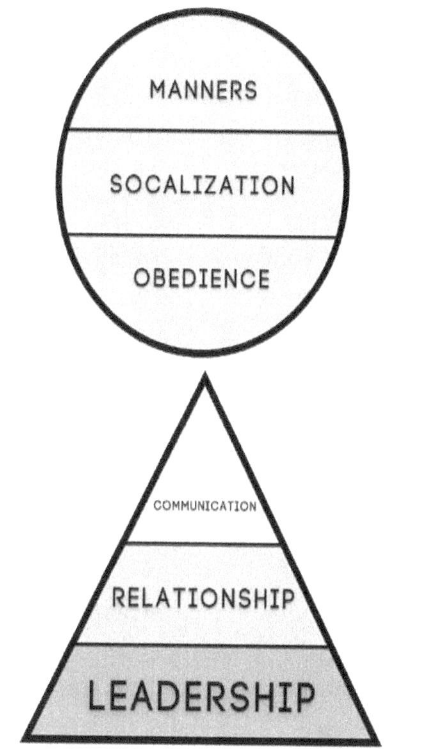

Diagram Number 3: The Leadership Pyramid Plus the Training Requirements Circle

Now, let's look again at our diagram number 3: As the pyramid shows, you need to get leadership right first. This is the foundation layer. Then, once you have established a solid relationship with your dog from the vantage point of that leadership, you are one level up. And then, right at the top of the pyramid, you have this amazing, clear communication between you and your dog. This pyramid is fertile ground for everything you want to undertake with your dog in the future. And it is always the same pyramid for every single dog, no matter what plans you may have for them: The same principles apply, whether you want a highly trained guard dog or just an amazingly dependable and obedient canine companion.

And yet, the pyramid is only the beginning: To get to the point where you have this perfect guard dog or companion dog, you also require the core training principles. In other words, you need what is in that circle that sits on top of the leadership-pyramid. And this circle has to be complete – you cannot have only one component of it and expect to get the ideal canine companion you want to have. In other words: For this (or any other) circle to be perfect, it has to be complete, smooth, even and well-rounded. Which means that all three training requirements must be fully present in equal measures: socialization, manners and obedience.

Now, you might fear that getting all these six different components established could be quite a challenge, especially if you had to slowly work your way up: first up the leadership-pyramid and then through the training requirements-circle. But worry not - you absolutely can work on the leadership-pyramid AND the training requirements simultaneously. If you do this - calmly and consistently - , you will be way ahead of the vast majority of dog owners. And you will be well on your way to having that dependable, well-mannered and obedient dog whom you want to have by your side. And whom you more than deserve, simply because you will have put in the effort, the discipline and the hard work that it takes to successfully raise a puppy.

So, once you have successfully built the pyramid, and you have come full circle with all three training requirements, you have achieved victory. You now have a perfect puppy that is well on its way to becoming the perfect canine companion of your dreams. And, basically, this is it - the ULTIMATE GOAL of puppy training!

And now, we are going to dive into the details of how exactly to achieve this lofty goal. In the following section, you will learn what are the most common mistakes on your road to puppy training victory – and how to avoid them.

Common Mistakes in Puppy Training

There are a few common mistakes that most people make in training dogs, especially when it comes to raising puppies. And if you find yourself "guilty" of any of them, please do not judge yourself - even experienced dog owners, and dog trainers, sometimes slip up in some of these areas. However, once you know what they are, you can very easily avoid these common mistakes in puppy training.

This in itself will help you and your dog immensely, simply because it is far easier to get things right in the first place, then to try and correct unruly behaviours later in your dog's life. Because, thankfully, most dogs grow up being great in most regards. And yet, there is usually this one little thing that they do that is either just annoying or downright dangerous. And their owners are mystified as to where this behaviour is even coming from. But, as the dog is wonderful in so many other ways, these owners do their best to just live with that one undesirable behaviour. This includes innocent quirks, but can go all the way up to aggressive outbursts that (seemingly) come from nowhere.

Why Avoiding these Mistakes is so Important

Unfortunately, unless corrected, these unwanted reactions oftentimes lead to serious behavioural issues that are very difficult to reverse. Especially when aggression is involved, a minor tendency to bark at other dogs on the street can lead to serious dog aggression in the long run. Because contrary to popular belief, aggression does not simply correct itself, and neither do puppies "grow out of it in time". Rather, aggression tends to escalate further, and if you have a big powerful dog on your hands, this can be a serious problem.

So, especially in more severe cases, owners often wait far too long before they intervene - or before they ask a canine behaviourist or trainer to intervene on their behalf. And I see this happen literally every day: Someone writes to me, saying something like this: "My Cane Corso has bitten my neighbour, and if he bites again, he will be put down. Can you help me save my dog's life, please?" Or, "My Rottweiler is trying to eat every dog we meet on our walks, and I can hardly hold him back. I'm afraid that one day, he will get loose and kill a smaller dog."

Of course, in each of those cases, I try my best to help that dog and its owner. But ultimately, once things have gone so far, the damage is done - and unraveling what went wrong is no easy feat. In such cases of seriously problematic behaviours like dogs attacking humans or other animals, it usually takes the help of an experienced expert to correct the behaviour and to straighten that dog out, so to speak. Once this has been achieved, the owners usually have to conclude that the cause of the problem was something *they* were doing – without even knowing that they were doing it.

It is for this reason that I have created my Perfect Puppy Program - a user-friendly video course that is basically an A - Z manual of how to train your young puppy. In this course, I cover everything discussed in this book in great depths, and illustrate it with real-life examples as well as precise guidance. And even though I would love to give you all the information contained in the course right now in these pages, it would by far exceed the format of this book: In essence, the book you are reading right now is a manual of puppy training principles and theories. The video course, on the other hand, is a detailed step-by-step program that shows you what to teach your puppy in each month of its life - all the way up to the 12 months mark. If you are interested in the Perfect Puppy Course, you can access it on my website,

https://www.fenrirdogtraining.com/courses.

If you do decide to get the Perfect Puppy Program, it is incredibly important that you follow it to the T, as this will allow you to raise your puppy to be a perfect canine companion. But even if you do, there still could be problem behaviours arising from things you are doing subconsciously. Which is why I am going to list the most common mistakes right here on the following pages.

These problems can be extremely difficult and expensive to correct once they have taken a foothold in your dog's psyche, which is why it is so important that you understand the overarching principles of puppy training. Because once you do, you can apply them to every scenario that may ever come up in the course of raising your puppy. And, even more importantly: Contrary to the average dog owner, *you* will have the skills to see those problems arising. You will have the confidence to tackle them straight away, and to stop those problem behaviours from happening in the first place. And that is precisely the key to being a high level canine leader. This ability to preempt problem-behaviours is the difference between an average dog trainer and owner and one of those excellent, outstanding ones that you will be one of!

Mistake Number 1 - Inconsistency

Inconsistency is the first common mistake that people make in training dogs – and it is a very common occurrence in raising puppies: Because young dogs are so incredibly cute, it is very easy to let them get away with things, or to ignore unwanted behaviours. Also, it is very tempting to skip training or socialisation sessions in favour of snuggles and cuddles. But this very common mistake can cause serious behavioural issues down the line. Therefore, you need to treat your puppy from day one just like you would treat an adult dog.

No matter how tempting it is to give in to those large, sad puppy eyes and to let your rules, boundaries and expectations slide just a little bit – stay strong! Always remember that dogs THRIVE on consistency, and on you being their calm, consistent leader. This empowers them to trust you and to always look to you for direction, which is imperative for having a safe, predictable dog. To feel secure, dogs have to know that they can count on you 100% of the time. And the easiest way for them to trust you is for you to be predictable and consistent. In every single detail.

Believe me, I know perfectly well just how hard this is from my own experience with raising puppies. But I assure you: If you stay strong and consistent, refusing to let your puppies get away with things, you set them up to succeed. And you will absolutely thank yourself for this in the years to come: Your self-discipline and perseverance will be amply rewarded by having a perfect canine companion by your side.

Mistake Number 2 - Anthropomorphization

Our next common mistake in raising puppies and training dogs is anthropomorphization. This essentially means that we attribute human emotions, characteristics or behaviours to our dogs. However, no matter how adorable puppies are or how much we love them - they still are dogs, and not humans. And in order to bring out the very best in them, we have to treat them as such. If we do, we are on the fast track to having this wonderful, almost psychic connection with them that we want to have.

But we must always remember that dogs do not think like we do. Their emotions are different from ours, and their responses to their environment are nothing like ours. Canines communicate extremely differently from us, and the more we understand this - and the more we interact with them as dogs, and not as humans -, the better we will be as their leaders. The better leader you are to your dog, the better relationship you will have with them - and ultimately, the better companion you will have as a result. If you just remember that dogs are dogs, and follow my principles (which are all informed by advanced canine psychology), you will be well on your way.

Mistake Number 3 - Training in a Bad Mood

Now, the next three mistakes I want to talk about are much easier to prevent: Once you know what they are, you can quickly catch yourself, and you will be back on track in no time at all. So, the first of these mistakes is training your puppy whilst you yourself are in a bad mood. Maybe you just had a bad day at work, an argument with your teenage son, or something happened that put you in a bad space. All this is completely understandable. But remember: Calm, consistent leadership is everything! Because if you are angry, stressed-out or wound up, and then you train your dog, you are setting BOTH of you up to fail. Therefore, take a minute, breathe, and calm yourself down first. Make sure you are in a good space before you continue your training session. In this way, you ensure that you yourself can be disciplined and consistent. Which will then bring about the excellent results you are looking for from your puppy.

Mistake Number 4 - Moving too fast

A very similar mistake to training in a bad mood is rushing things. Which is why, in my Perfect Puppy Course, I have broken down most of my modules into stages. To illustrate what I mean, let's briefly look at the example of heel-training: We start off with zero distractions, which means we teach our puppy to walk nicely to heel inside of our house. Then, once they have grasped what we are asking them to do, we proceed to the garden. And only after our puppy is showing us good and solid heel-work in the garden, do we take them outside of our property. From there onwards, we gradually increase the level of distractions as we progress in our heel-work. However, we only move on after our puppy has mastered the previous stage to 100%.

Because oftentimes, owners who move too fast in their training, end up blaming their dogs and becoming angry with them. They might even punish them for "failing", which is not only unnecessary, but downright counterproductive. However, had these owners not rushed their puppies in the first place, they would have been just fine.

Young dogs are sensitive beings, and sometimes they are simply not ready to move on to the next stage of their training. Therefore, if a puppy "fails", the mistake is always with the owner. So, take your time and be happy with what you have achieved before moving on. And if you catch yourself having moved too quickly, do not worry, and do not punish the dog or get angry. Instead, just stay calm and consistent, and move back a step. In our example of teaching Heel, this could mean you stop asking your puppy to heel in a public setting, and instead, you continue perfecting their performance inside your garden or backyard. Then, celebrate and reward that success - with praise, play or treats. In this way, you end each training session (and each training stage) on a positive note and with zero stress on either yourself or your puppy.

Mistake Number 5 - Reinforcing Bad Habits

And the last main mistake in puppy training is reinforcing bad habits by accident. This is a common result of anthropomorphizing our dogs. For example, if our puppy is afraid of large lorries rumbling past them on the street, we naturally want to comfort them like we would a young child. So, we give them affection as soon as they flinch or jump. In this way, we unwittingly reinforce their fear.

But how can we avoid this - very human and understandable - response of trying to comfort our puppy when it is scared? The answer is quite simple: Rather than reacting to the undesirable response (such as flinching), we always want to model and reinforce the *desired* behaviour. So, in our example with the loud and scary lorry, we would completely ignore that negative response, and instead model calm, relaxed behaviour for our puppy. And we praise and reward them once they, too, are calm and relaxed.

An excellent way to go about this is doing your obedience work whilst a lorry is approaching. In this way, we can keep our dog's focus on something else, and we already have them look to us for direction. Whenever their attention moves to this offensive lorry, ignore the fear, but encourage your puppy to return its focus to you, and to the obedience work at hand. Then praise and reward the puppy once its attention is back where it should be.

So, avoiding the common mistake of reinforcing bad habits is quite simple. Just remember to ALWAYS PRAISE AND REWARD DESIRED BEHAVIOURS – and to NEVER GIVE ATTENTION, PRAISE OR REWARD FOR UNDESIRABLE BEHAVIOURS. If you catch yourself rewarding fearful, anxious or hyperactive behaviour, simply stop, take a breath, and flip the script - before any unwanted behaviour has a chance to take root in the mind of your puppy.

We want Impeccable Manners

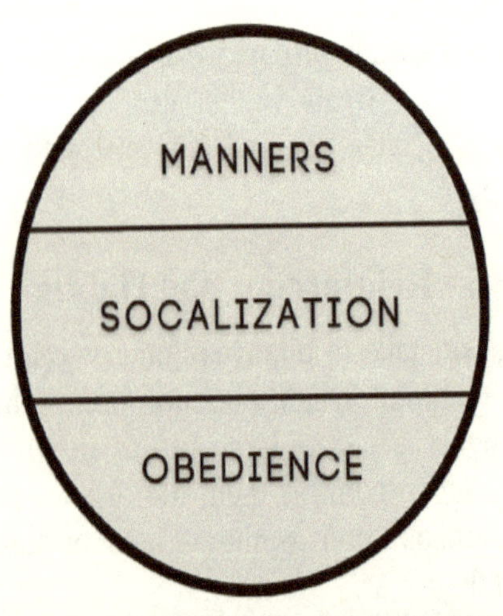

Diagram Number 4: Circle of Core Training Principles

In the following section of our book, we will look at the training-principles in greater detail. However, as we have limited space in this book, I cannot possibly give you all the little details of how to lead your puppy from one step to the other. But what I will do right here, right now, is give you the overarching principles of what I teach in the course. And this knowledge alone will enable you to raise perfect puppies, simply because you will have grasped the core basics of dog training. And with that crucial knowledge under your belt, you will be more than able to tackle the day-to-day tasks involved in raising and training your puppy. Let's begin!

In my personal opinion, manners are of the utmost importance when it comes to harmoniously living together with dogs. Simply because there is nothing worse than having a loud, obnoxious dog whose deafening barks are a daily annoyance to yourself and your neighbours. Or think about all the dogs you know who jump up on people, lunge at other dogs or regularly clear the coffee table with their tails, simply because they have never learned to behave well. You might think that obedience training would automatically fix these behaviours, but oftentimes it fails to do so. Teaching out-of-control canines commands may keep them in a Down & Stay-position for a few minutes, if you are lucky, but after that, they will jump right back into overdrive. Therefore, obedience training in and by itself will not do *anything* to make a chaotic canine into a dog who is pleasant to live with.

So, now that we have clearly stated what we do NOT want, we can move on to what we DO want from our dogs in the field of manners: Our aim is having a dog who is extremely polite towards strangers, meeting and greeting them in a calm, relaxed and well-mannered way. A dog who does not jump up at people, but will patiently and quietly look for our directions. The dog of our dreams is an immensely well-mannered individual who will *always* respect the boundaries that we as their leaders set for them. Such a dog will be calm and patient, also in your absence: Whenever you need to go out, they will be quietly waiting for your return. Without howling, crying or destroying your house whilst you are away. If feeding time comes around, but you are busy doing something else, such a dog will politely wait its turn.

The 3-Step Process for Perfect Puppy-Behaviour

So, we have stated what we clearly do not want, as well as what we do want from our dogs when it comes to manners. Now, in order to get the impeccably mannered dog, you do not need any kind of harsh correction. You only need to adopt our 3-Step Process for Perfect Puppy-Behaviour - ideally, from the very first day onwards. But if you have "missed the boat" and your youngster is already slightly older than eight weeks, do not despair. Simply take the following steps:

1. Establish clear, consistent boundaries
2. Praise and reward good manners
3. Challenge bad manners

Of course, challenging bad manners does not mean yelling at your dog or beating them into compliance. It can be as simple as removing your attention from the dog, and completely ignoring its behaviour. Or it can be giving a verbal correction to break your puppy's focus (for example on biting your shoe-laces), and to bring that focus back to you. Then, you redirect the dog to the positive, desired behaviour you want them to display. In our example of biting shoe-laces, that could mean we encourage them to bite a chew-toy instead. Then - as soon as your puppy sinks its little teeth into that chew-toy - , you reinforce this behaviour with lots of praise. Whenever you do this, timing is of the essence: You want to be lightning-fast in your reactions, both to the unwanted and to the wanted behaviour.

If you make following this 3-Step Process a habit, you are setting yourself and your puppy up to succeed - straight from the start: Because you are getting things right in the first place, you do not need to use punitive tools later on in your journey. And neither do you need to spend fortunes on dog trainers to come in and fix (very complex and established) bad behaviours: With this simple 3-Step Process, you will save yourself years of heartache and thousands of dollars.

As we saw before in the "Common Mistakes"-section of this chapter, the biggest challenge when it comes to puppy training is accidentally reinforcing bad behaviour - in this case, bad manners. For example, if you greet your dog excitedly when you come back home, you can cause them to develop separation anxiety. But as you are reading this book, you will not fall prey to this all too understandable mistake. Instead, you will stay calm as you walk into that door, completely ignoring your dog until it, too, has calmed down. Then, you will praise and reward that calm behaviour. And before too long, you will have a dog who is calm, relaxed and patient - simply because he has learned that being calm gets him what he wants. Such a dog actively seeks to be calm, as he knows that this is how he earns praise, attention and rewards. In this way, your dog will thrive, and always seek to act in a well-mannered way.

The Importance of Exercise

Even though this book is not an exercise-guide for puppies, the fact remains: Dogs of all ages are much more likely to be in that ideal calm, relaxed state of mind when they are tired. A tired dog is a good dog! Of course, you should always consult your vet when it comes to how much exercise is good for your puppy - and how much is too much. Because whilst wild dogs and wolves romp around all day, unsupervised by vets and owners, many of our modern breeds could suffer injuries, or even lasting deformities, if exercised too much during puppyhood. This applies mostly to breeds (and mixed-breeds) whose size and shape are considerably removed from their original form - the wolf.

Common examples for such dogs are Dachshunds and Bassets, whose vastly elongated backs are prone to injury. Or Mastiffs and other giant breeds: Being unnaturally large and heavy, puts a lot of strain on their joints. They also take up to three years to fully mature: If you exercise Mastiff puppies too much, they can damage the growth plates in their joints, which can cause quite painful problems later in their lives.

Therefore, you want to exercise caution when it comes to exercising your puppy. But after you have checked with your vet how much playtime and walking-time your puppy should have, make sure you give it to them. Without a doubt, you will thank yourself for doing so, because exercise in itself is a magical key to unlocking the treasure trove of desirable behaviours: A young dog who has the chance to burn off excess energy on a regular basis is much less likely to display "naughty" behaviours - such as chewing, puppy biting or jumping around in the house. At the same time, exercising your dog has countless benefits for strengthening that all-important bond between the both of you. And as an added bonus, engaging your canine companion in play sessions and walks gives you the chance to be out and about more. In this way, you will get more exercise yourself, out there in the fresh air of nature, whilst spending quality time with your dog.

We Need Superb Socialization

In the circle of core training principles, socialization sits sandwiched between manners and obedience. Which is quite a fitting place, as it is intimately connected to both of them: A well-socialised dog will have a much easier timebeing calm, reliable and well-behaved than a socially insecure one. Which means such a dog will be calm and confident enough to be receptive to any commands you might want to give them. And having learned that calm, relaxed behaviour gets them what they want, they will display good manners.

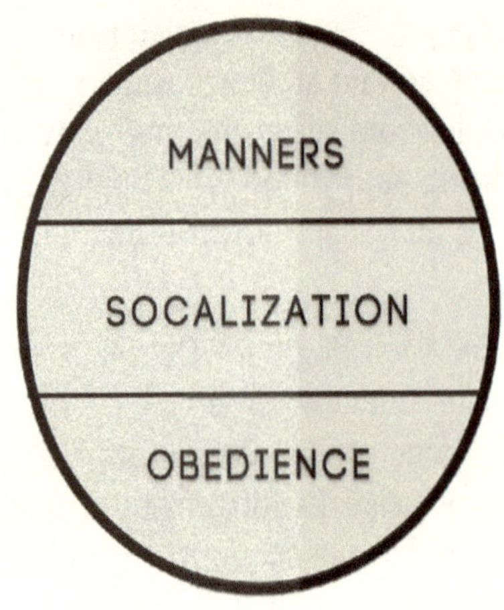

Diagram Number 4: Circle of Core Training Principles

This is how these three core training principles are connected. Let's illustrate this with an example. If you have put in all the effort required to adequately socialize your puppy, you will have an amazing, calm and confident dog by your side once that puppy has grown up. So, assuming that this is the case, let's say you are out walking your dog, and a car pulls up right next to you. The driver scrolls down his window, waves a large paper roadmap in the air and asks you for directions. You step closer to the car so you can look onto the map. Your dog - who had been walking nicely to heel on a loose leash - quietly follows, then sits down next to you (taking your stopping as the clue to assume a Sit & Stay position). You then take the map, see where the driver wants to go and give him appropriate directions. He thanks you sund drives off. Then, you turn your attention back to the dog, reward him with "Good boy!" and a gentle pat on the head - and continue your walk.

This is what an ideal scenario looks like. Now, IF that dog had not been socialized, he would have gotten spooked or alarmed by that car pulling up right next to you. Maybe he would have flinched, retreated and even tried to slip out of his collar. Or he might have started barking and lunging towards the car - either in an aggressive or in a playful manner. What this dog would NOT have done, however, is calmly keeping up the heel-position and falling into a relaxed Sit & Stay: Even if the dog was impeccably trained in obedience and manners, he would have become too rattled by the car coming so close (and the driver wafting his map in front of his owner's face) to assume a calm, seated position.

Of course, barking and lunging at cars and people is just one of the many potential behavioural problems that owners have to face. But they all have one thing in common: They could have been stopped from happening in the first place - had the dog simply been better socialised.

But as a general rule of thumb, we want to socialize our puppies to as many things, places, people, animals and situations as possible. In this way, we create as many positive associations to those different environments, people and objects as we can. This is a big part of setting our puppies up to succeed. Because as they get older, they will be much less likely to freak out, slip out of their collars and run off if a car pulls up right next to them and some sort of strange object is being waved in front of their faces. Like that roadmap in our example. Also, if they are socialized to other dogs from an early age onwards, they are less likely to become aggressive when another dog comes running towards them.

As a rule of thumb, you want to familiarise your puppy with everything that they will most likely have to face in their lives. Examples for this include rides in your car, car-parks, dog parks, vet-visits, busy roads, crowded pedestrian zones, motorcycles, bicycles, busses, and so forth. Of course, you want to ensure that your puppy meets as many friendly dogs and humans as possible.

If you are raising your dog for a very specific role, then you absolutely would emphasise this in your socialization schedule. For example, your puppy's future role might be to guard your cattle, to herd your flock of sheep, or to protect your chickens from predators. In these cases, you absolutely want to socialise your puppy with the animals whom it will be around later. Not only the animals whom it will have to guard, but also the other species present on your farm. Doing this from a young age onwards is crucial, not only to allow your dog to deeply bond with the animals in question, but also to avoid accidents later. Such as an overzealous sheepdog with a high prey drive (like a Border Collie or a working line German Shepherd) ripping into your chickens.

And the same principle applies if you want your dog to accompany you on a very specialized hobby. Let's say that your favourite thing to do is going on fishing trips in your boat. In this case, you would spend more time socializing your puppy to lakes, the sea, your boat and fishing line etc. If you are an avid hunter, you would acquaint your puppy to the sight and smell of your rifle and your gear, as well as to the sound of shots fired. You would take them along on hunting trips simply to observe and get familiar with what is going on from an early age onwards.

But whatever your situation may be, you can use the very same principles for introducing something new to your puppy. The standard technique is quite simple and straightforward: Basically, we introduce your puppy to the new object, environment, animal or person of our choice. Then, we do one of two things:

1. If our puppy responds in a calm, confident and positive manner, we praise and reward them.
2. If our puppy responds in a fearful, negative or anxious manner, we stay calm, ignore those behaviors and move back a step.

So, let's assume you live out in the countryside and you walk your young puppy past your neighbor's horse corral for the first time. At first, all seems well, but suddenly, your puppy realises that there are some large animals in that corral. Animals that now start slowly moving towards the dog. Quite understandably, your puppy tries to flee, pulling away from the corral in an attempt to avoid those menacing animals. So, what to do? As you will have read this book, you will avoid the common mistake that 99% of dog owners would commit in such a situation - which is trying to comfort your puppy, petting it and telling it "Ooh, you poor thing, it's okay!" Instead, you completely ignore your dog's fearful behaviour, instead calmly moving forward until you are past that corral.

But on the next day, you will take your puppy back to the scene of that fearful reaction. Just not quite as close as before: Together with your puppy, you would simply watch those horses from a distance. Here is where good leadership comes in - by modelling calm, confident behaviour, you signal to your dog that everything is okay, and once they, too, are calm in the face of the horses grazing away at a safe distance, you instantly praise and reward that good behaviour. Now is a great time to give your puppy a nice treat, especially if it has assumed a Sit & Stay position whilst watching the horses from a comfortable distance. In this way, you create positive associations with those horses. Then, once your puppy has confidently mastered the art of horse-watching, you build back up to walking right past the corral slowly, one step at a time.

Socialization is not all that difficult, but it does require commitment and discipline: It is often easier to just take our puppies around the block on a familiar route, where they will not be exposed to many different things that can make them feel afraid - like lots of traffic, people milling about and other dogs barking at them from behind fences. But as tempting as it is to "take it easy" when it comes to socializing our puppies, it is not a good idea. Simply because once the damage is done, it is very hard – and sometimes impossible – to undo. For example, if you miss the critical socialization periods that we have discussed in Chapter 2, you could have an insecure dog on your hands that is afraid of its own shadow.

This in fact often happens in rural areas, where people hardly walk their dogs. Instead, they hook them up to a chain - or, in the best case, put them into a fenced area - and expect them to protect their property. These dogs almost never see other dogs or humans, let alone cars, busses or motorbikes. And as these puppies grow up, they often stay insecure outside of their (very limited) comfort zone, no matter how hard any future owner - or dog trainer - tries to correct the fearful behaviour.

So, whenever you think you have put in sufficient effort on the socialization front, remember that you do not want to miss these windows of opportunity. So, if in doubt, better to err on the side of caution - and to socialize your puppy to as many things as possible: objects, situations, circumstances, procedures, people and animals. No matter how ridiculous some of these things may seem. Because the more seemingly random things your puppy is socialized to, the less likely it is to freak out at something it was *not* socialized to. So, if your dog encounters some unlikely object (like a bouncy castle suddenly appearing on the marketplace), it will not be rattled, because it will have encountered lots of weird and random things before. Instead, your dog will look to you for direction on how to respond, and because you are a calm, consistent leader in the face of that bouncy castle, your dog will be happy to follow your lead.

And lastly, as long as your puppy has not received all its vaccinations, you need to exercise caution when it comes to socializing them. Always check with your vet first before you take your puppy out into the public.

CHAPTER 2

Why BASIC Obedience is Enough

Now, we come to the third and last section of the circle of core training principles - obedience. And it is important to remember that obedience is only one third of what it takes to have a perfect canine companion. Manners and especially socialization are equally - if not more! - important. Simply because you can always work on your dog's obedience, no matter their age, but you cannot possibly bring back those socialization stages of early puppyhood. So, if you find yourself slightly overwhelmed with having a new puppy and everything that comes with it - obedience is the one aspect of puppy training that can wait. Again, manners are much more important, simply because they make living with your new dog on a day-to-day basis so much easier.

For example, let's say the first thing your new puppy learns is to sink its teeth into its chew-toy - instead of into your hands. Even if this is all the young dog learns in the first few weeks in terms of good manners: This alone puts you well ahead of your fellow puppy owners whose dogs still bite them whenever they feel like it - but already can perform Sit, Down and Heel. Because by successfully redirecting puppy biting, you have already established clear leadership in the relationship you have with your dog.

These other owners might not have. Simply because dogs do not mouth their leaders. But you do not need to take my word for it: Jump on YouTube and watch those video clips that show how mother dogs correct their pups! This is very educational, and I highly recommend you watch exactly how these naturally calm, consistent canine leaders deal with unruly offspring. No puppy would dream about teething and snapping at their mother, let alone about biting down in a painful manner, like so many puppies do with their owners. Therefore, again, if you have only mastered this one aspect of manners, you are well ahead of the vast majority of puppy owners.

My 6 Non-Negotiables of Obedience Training

But with that said - of course, obedience is important. And for dogs to be safe in every situation, they need to have mastered at least basic obedience. Personally, I am not a huge fan of elaborate obedience drills, mainly because a few short and simple commands are enough for me to have my dog under control at all times.

Recall

And one of these commands is recall. In my case, I use my whistle for this, so two short pips on that whistle signals to my dog that I want them right here by my side. From this position, I can quickly and comfortably secure them with a leash and continue my walk. But you can also choose any kind of verbal cue to teach recall, preferably preceded by your dog's name. So, for example, you could call "Max, Come!", to first get your dog's attention and then to instruct Max to stop what he was doing and return to you immediately.

Recall can easily save a dog's life, which is why I regard this as the single most important command your dog will ever learn. For example, let's say you are outside in your garden, tending to your vegetable plot. And whilst you are working, your spouse has opened the gate, because they are preparing to leave the property in their car. Max, your trusted canine companion, is by your side, taking a nap in the grass. But suddenly, Max hears another dog barking and yapping right outside that open gate. Alarmed, Max jumps to his feet and starts running toward that open gate, right towards the busy street outside. Instantly, you shout your command for recall ("Max, Come!"), and Max stops, turns around and comes running back towards you.

Evidently - and luckily for everyone involved -, Max is an obedient dog: A dog that is under control in all scenarios, and that is a pleasure to live with. An obedient dog is a safe dog, simply because it is always under its owner's control. Just like your dependable Max. Such a dog also is safe for everyone around them: You can trust them to always follow your guidance. A dog like Max will not just blindly lunge at other dogs, trying to bite them, or wildly jump up at people coming to visit, almost knocking them over in the process.

Apart from recall, there are five other commands that I teach my puppies. Which is not all that much, but in my personal experience, it is more than enough for a perfect canine companion. I call these six basic commands "The Non-Negotiables", and I highly suggest that you embrace them as well and teach them to your puppy. Once your dog has mastered all of these six "Non-Negotiables", it will have become a perfect canine companion in the field of obedience: These six commands underpin everything else you ever might want to teach your dog. After you have mastered them, you can take obedience training as far as you want to take it.

Your Dog's Name

By the time you bring your puppy home, you will probably already have chosen a name for it. And teaching your dog its name is something you can start doing right from the get-go - before you even delve into recall and all the other basic commands I will get into in this section.

Think of your dog's name as the foundation to everything: As we saw in our example of you in your garden, calling Max back, the first word you uttered to get his attention was his name - then, after that, you used a command that told him what to do. In that case, it was to return to your side, but it can be anything.

But in teaching and using our dogs' names, we must again resist the temptation to project human attributes onto our dogs: Whilst we very much identify with our given name, and think of ourselves as this specific person whom the world knows as "Tom", "John" or "Mary", dogs do not do this. So, if your canine companion Max sees your neighbour's dog, Spot the Dachshund, he does not think, "Oh, there goes Spot, leaving the house for his morning walk." Rather, "Spot" is a specific scent, combined with a visual impression. Some say, dogs perceive each other as energy, or as a combination of scent, sight and sound. But they certainly do not think of each other as Max or Spot.

So, when we teach our new puppy the name we have selected for them, we are teaching them to associate that word with a very specific meaning: When you call "Max!", you want your dog to shift his attention to you. You want Max to look towards you and listen out for the next clue. In other words, you have taught your puppy that you calling "Max!" means : "Pay attention to me for direction, because I'm about to give you further guidance, or ask something of you."

"Sit"

As we said, teaching your dog its name is a command, and it simply means, "Look up to me for guidance and direction, because I am about to give you more information." Once your puppy understands that, you are on the fast track to having an obedient dog. Because now, you can tag on pretty much any command you want. And many owners teach a basic recall-command right after teaching the name, and a simple "Come" will usually do. What I personally like to teach next is "Sit" - an extremely straight-forward, but wonderfully useful tool for obedience, socialisation and manners!

"Sit" will probably be the most common command that you are going to use with your dog. Personally, I use Sit for all household manners that I want to teach my puppy. For example, I condition them to sit before they get their food, their time on the sofa, their toy and so forth. Sit is an incredibly effective tool for building up the relationship with your dog. A solid mastery of this simple basic command can work wonders in keeping your dog safe, and in allowing you to very easily work on their manners.

"Stay"

The next non-negotiable command I like to teach is "Stay", which is a perfect addition to "Sit". It is also incredibly important for our dog's safety. To illustrate this, let's once again assume your loyal canine companion, Max, is running off. This time, you are out walking him in the fields behind your house. Thanks to Max's flawless recall, you can let him run off leash every day. But as it happens, during today's walk, Max's attention is caught by a hare that suddenly jumps up ahead of him and darts off into the distance. Following his natural impulse to give chase, Max leaps after the hare - straight towards the railway track at the edge of the field.

Immediately, you shout "Max - Stay!", and fortunately, your dog's training kicks in, he stops dead in his tracks and stays still, waiting for your next command, which probably will be "Come!"

So, what you have just successfully done is you have called your dog's name, which he knew to mean: "STOP and look to me for direction!". You followed this up with a "Stay", meaning, "I need you to stay right where you are." Max does not know why he has to break off his hunt, but because he trusts you as his calm, consistent leader, he complies with your command.

The tremendous power of "Sit & Stay", a combo which also allows you to easily work on leadership and manners. For example, when your puppy's meal time comes around, you can use "Sit & Stay" to teach them impulse control. To do this, you simply have them sit and stay before allowing them to eat their food. This only takes one minute of your time, but it greatly enhances both your leadership and your puppy's manners. In this way, you can take advantage of everyday situations and use them to reinforce rules and boundaries within your home and your family. As this example shows, teaching puppies does not need to be a time-consuming endeavor.

"Leave it" & "Break"

Two other basic obedience principles that I have found vastly useful in working with dogs are "Leave it" and "Break". "Leave it" is an extremely important thing to teach, because - much like recall - , it can save your dog's life. Especially during their puppyhood: Puppies seem to come up with endless ways to endanger themselves, and if you have ever raised one, you will know exactly what I am talking about. And if you are right now planning to get your very first puppy, this is something to keep in mind. Of course, diligently puppy-proofing your home and garden is one important measure to take before bringing your new dog home. But what if you catch them in the act of picking up or chewing something that could harm them - like a strand of ivy, another dog's poop or your computer cable? In these cases, "Leave it" can be a true life-saver. "Leave it" basically means "Drop whatever it is you've got in your mouth right away!"

The "Break" command is not quite as dramatic, but I like teaching it to puppies, as it helps them to avoid confusion - and it helps their owners to communicate clearly with them. "Break" can be combined with pretty much any command you ask of your puppy, no matter how advanced. It simply means that this command is now over, and the dog is free to resume its normal activities. It is a very clear way of communicating with your dog, far easier than "muddling up your commands", so to speak, by demanding your dog "Sit & Stay", then walking away and having them break the stay whenever they see fit.

Such a thing, of course, should be avoided, but you need one good clue that tells your dog that they are free to stop performing that command. Usually, people use something like "Good boy!", Let's go!" or "Come on!" to relieve their dogs from commands like "Sit", "Stay" or "Down", but that can *create* confusion - whereas "Break" *removes* any confusion. Which means that you become an even more consistent leader to your dog - and that means that you have an even better canine companion!

"Heel"

And the sixth and last basic obedience command I teach is "Heel". I am a great fan of having dogs walk nicely to heel, even though I do not usually train dogs to competition-levels in the field of obedience. The reason why I like "Heel" so much is that it allows me - and my clients - to enjoy every walk with our dogs to the fullest.

Again, I do not teach and use "Heel" to competition-standards, so the dog does not have to walk with his nose glued to my pocket. All I want is a dog who will walk next to me on a loose lead, nicely and calmly, for however long I ask them to. They can lag a little bit behind or be slightly to the front, but they hold the heel-position until I ask them to break.

This may not seem too spectacular, but walking your dog like this is an experience that can transform living with them, especially for owners who used to get pulled every which way by their unruly canines. For many of such owners, walking their dogs is a chore. Whereas with good heel-walking in place, taking your dog for walks can easily become the highlight and the joy of your day.

Of course, if you have a Pekinese or a Dachshund on your leash, pulling and yanking is not as much of a problem as for owners of big, powerful Mastiff-type breeds: If those dogs uncontrollably pull on the lead, walking them becomes next to impossible. Which then means people walk them less, so these muscular dogs get far less exercise than they should get. And far less than they need to stay balanced and well-rounded. Which then leads to an escalation of other unwanted behaviours, such as aggressively lunging at other dogs. In this way, leash-pulling can be the first step down a very slippery slope. But the descent into the darkness of owning a badly behaved dog can as easily be avoided by teaching that dog how to walk nicely to heel. Therefore, you absolutely want to put in the time and effort needed to teach your puppy a good "Heel" - especially if you are planning to get a big powerful breed.

However, walking to heel on a loose leash can benefit any dog: A 140 pound-Mastiff as well as a 10 pound-Poodle. Simply because having your dog right by your side further strengthens their bond with you. In essence, walking to heel means keeping that leash loose. And to do that, your dog needs to pay attention to you. They have to look up to you for guidance and direction, as you turn left or right, navigate pedestrian traffic and stop before crossing a road. This alone will work wonders in emphasising your leadership.

Walking your dog in this way will automatically establish healthy habits in their mind, such as to always look to you for guidance, to adjust their pace, and to sit and stay whenever you stop walking etc. And these habits will then extend to any other situation that may come up in the future. As habits are formed by repetition, this is an example of nature working for you, establishing automatic behavioural patterns in your dog - in this case, very desirable ones.

But the opposite also applies: If you allow your dog to be out in front during your walks, pulling on the leash, then they are essentially leading you, not the other way around. Which of course is very counterproductive for establishing and maintaining good leadership. Because now, they are not looking for guidance from you, but instead, they make their own decisions: about where to turn to, what to sniff at, whom to bark at and so forth. Again, habits form by default if an action is repeated often enough, and letting your dog lead you is not a pattern you want to establish in your puppy's highly receptive mind.

And this brings us to the end of our discussion of my personal 6 non-negotiable training commands that I highly recommend you use for your puppy. In the following chapters, we will dive deeply into the hands-on practise of teaching these commands to your puppy. The methods we will use for this are usually just combinations of luring and positive reinforcement. (Luring basically means using a treat to lead the dog into a new position (like Sit or Down) for the first time.) Myself, I like to use treats and praise as rewards, and gradually move towards praise alone, as the dog gets more familiar with the new command. But if your puppy responds better to play than to food, then by all means, use play as reward.

PART 4

RAISING PERFECT PUPPIES A – Z

In the previous section, we have focused on the core principles of puppy training. And we have seen how *leadership, relationship and communication* tie into the three pillars of puppy training: *socialization, manners and obedience*.

Once we combine all of these elements, the reward for our efforts is at our fingertips. And that reward is to have this perfect puppy we have always wanted - the amazing canine companion of our dreams. Then, as time goes on (and we keep up our good work), this perfect puppy will grow into an obedient, well-socialized and well-behaved adult. Contrary to most owners, we will have a dog who looks to us for guidance and direction in all situations. We have seen how we can avoid the most common mistakes people make in training puppies. And we have discussed how to teach our young dogs basic commands.

Which leads us straight into Part 4 of our book Jam-packed with valuable information, this section is broken down into 4 different chapters. Here, we cover just about everything that you need to know about raising perfect puppies. We begin with an entire chapter dedicated to operant conditioning. If you have never heard of operant conditioning, do not worry: Cryptical as the term may sound, the principle behind it is quite easy and straightforward. After discussing what operant conditioning is (and how we can use it for training our dogs), we will then delve into the magical 90:10 rule of dog training. From there onwards, we will ponder the question which kinds of reinforcements and corrections are appropriate to use for our dogs. After that, we will discuss how to communicate with our dogs - without even needing words. And at the end of Part 4, you will find little-known secrets to socializing your puppy. Let's begin!

socializing your puppy. Let's begin!

CHAPTER 1

Operant Conditioning for Dog Owners

The term *operant conditioning* was coined in the year 1937 by the American Psychologist B.F. Skinner. In essence, operant conditioning is an associative learning process. The core purpose of this process is to *modify the frequency of a certain behaviour.* And the tools used to achieve this modification are reinforcement and punishment. To this day, this process is being employed all over the world, by therapists, teachers – and dog trainers! Because even though operant conditioning has been designed by a Psychologist, it is the foundation of all learning: Both for humans and for the majority of animals, including dogs.

Just like humans, dogs learn by means of operant conditioning. And literally every interaction that we have with our dogs takes place in one of the four areas of operant conditioning. The more we understand this almost universal learning mechanism, the more success we will achieve in raising and training our puppies. Used in this way, operant conditioning is an incredible tool for teaching our dogs what we want them to do.

Unfortunately, most owners do not understand their dogs' ways of learning. And this lack of understanding can cause a huge array of behavioural issues. By using their dogs' learning mechanism in the wrong way, these owners program problematic behaviours straight into their dogs. In this way, they *make* them misbehave - instead of training them to become the perfect canine companions they want. And then, they react in ways which perpetuate these unwanted behaviours. This is exactly why so many dogs suffer from severe behavioural problems, even though their owners have only their best interest at heart.

As with everything in life, there is a learning curve, and it is natural to make mistakes. Even for dog trainers and behaviourists. But if we take a step back, learn from our mistakes, and *then* return to training our dogs, we set ourselves up to succeed. And operant conditioning can help us on our journey to success: Once we have gained a clear understanding of operant conditioning, our interactions with your dogs will be much smoother than before. And we will be on the fast track to puppy training success. This goes far beyond "just" having an amazingly obedient dog, because excellent obedience is a mere by-product of the process. What is far more important is that we will have a well-rounded dog who is content, confident and happy. A dog who is in harmony with itself, with us as their leader, and with their environment. So, without further delay, let's jump into the fascinating realm of operant conditioning – and let's see how we can use it to maximise our puppy training success.

The 4 Areas of Operant Conditioning

(1) POSITIVE REINFORCEMENT	(2) NEGATIVE REINFORCEMENT
(3) POSITIVE PUNISHMENT	(4) NEGATIVE PUNISHMENT

Diagram Number 5: The Four Areas of Operant Conditioning.

In operant conditioning, we have 4 different areas. These are divided into 2 segments for reinforcement, and another 2 for punishment. For each of those, we have a "positive" and a "negative". Now, the problem with the terms "positive" and "negative" is: As soon as we read them, our mind invariably associates them with certain images and scenarios. Such as dogs being punished harshly by heartless trainers. Our mind's eye shows us innocent puppies being beaten, yanked about on leashes, strangled with choke-collars, etc.

But this is not what we mean when we use the terms "positive" and "negative" in the context of operant conditioning: Here, *"positive" and "negative" do not mean "good" and "bad"!* And in the same way, "punishment" is not necessarily what you would think it is: "Punishment" does not mean we impose any kind of correction (verbal or physical). It simply means we take measures *to see a behaviour happen LESS frequently.* Just like "Reinforcement" means we take measures *to see a behaviour happen MORE frequently.*

And this is really the essence of all dog training - no matter what school of thought we are following: the gentle positive-only approach, the harsher dominance-based approach or, like myself, the balanced approach. We all want our dogs to display desirable behaviours more often (like sitting down on command). And also, we want them to display *undesirable* behaviours *less* often (like jumping up on people). Now, in order to achieve that, we use "positive" and "negative" measures. Again, in this context, this has *nothing* to do with "good" or "bad": "Positive" quite simply means "to add something into the equation". And "negative" means "to remove something from the equation".

So, we have our 4 areas of operant conditioning: (1) Positive Reinforcement, (2) Negative Reinforcement, (3) Positive Punishment and (4) Negative Punishment. When we apply Positive Reinforcement, we are *adding* something in, for a behaviour to be seen more often. And when we apply Negative Reinforcement, we are *removing* something from the dog – again, to see the behaviour more often. When we apply Positive Punishment, we are again adding something in, with the aim of decreasing the frequency of a behaviour. And in Negative Punishment, we are removing something from the dog, aiming to, again, decrease the frequency of the behaviour. Therefore, "Positive" means TO ADD. And "Negative" means TO REMOVE. Reinforcement means a behaviour is going to be seen MORE frequently, and Punishment means a behaviour is going to be seen LESS frequently.

These 4 sections of operant conditioning contain all the tools we have in our arsenal. And equipped with a clear understanding of those tools, we can reach amazing levels of success. In my personal experience, using operant conditioning in a balanced way is the shortcut to shaping puppies into wonderful canine companions.

Now, I totally understand that the terms used in operant conditioning can be quite confusing. For this reason, we will now dive into each section in detail. And we will see how we can use operant conditioning in our day-to-day life with our dogs. So, let's jump straight into the depths of operant conditioning for dog owners!

1) Positive Reinforcement

And we begin with Positive Reinforcement (*adding something into the equation, for a behaviour to be seen more often*). One classical example for using Positive Reinforcement is giving your dog a treat for a job well done: You say, "Bella, Sit!", your dog sits down, and you give her a piece of sausage.

In this short, simple interaction with Bella, she has shown you a desirable behaviour - in this case, sitting down on command. And as you would like to see this behaviour more often in the future, you wanted to *reinforce* it. For this reason, you have added something (*positive*) into the equation: the piece of sausage. In this manner, you have just successfully applied Positive Reinforcement.

There is no doubt about it: Positive Reinforcement is a wonderful tool, and you can get as creative as you want in utilizing it. Also, it is very time-efficient: You can easily integrate Positive Reinforcement into your everyday routines with your dog. And you can use it to enhance leadership, relationship and communication.

You can start positively reinforcing your puppy right from the start: Even an eight week old puppy is receptive to this gentle approach to training. One great way to apply this is at your puppy's mealtimes. The ritual of preparing their food and giving it to them only takes a few minutes. But if you use those few minutes wisely, your puppy will learn basic lessons in manners and obedience right from their first day in your household.

The process in itself is quite easy: Every time you are ready to put the food bowl down in front of your puppy, hold on for a moment. Stand quietly, bowl in hand, and simply wait until your puppy sits down and looks up to you. This will happen sooner or later, even if they initially jump and whine, eager to get their food. Then, once they are in a calm sitting position, you put the food bowl onto the floor and let them eat their well-earned meal.

No matter which breed of dog you might have, I guarantee you they will "connect the dots" quite quickly: After a few repetitions of this feeding ritual, your puppy will understand: "Okay, if I sit down and wait calmly, I get my food." Dogs are very smart. And once they have associated something they really want with sitting and waiting, they will want to repeat this behaviour more often. (By the way, this is also one of the easiest methods to teach the basic command-sequence "Sit & Stay".)

As this example shows, Positive Reinforcement is a wonderful tool. But at the same time, this is also the area where the most mistakes are made. Because the majority of well-meaning dog owners unwittingly use Positive Reinforcement the wrong way around - accidentally enforcing unruly behaviours, such as chewing, barking, or jumping up on people.

Let's take barking for example. Imagine a scenario where you live in an apartment - together with your dog "Teddy", an adorable adolescent Golden Retriever. You are sitting at your desk, fully immersed in the task of writing an email on your computer. In the corner next to your desk, Teddy is peacefully snoring away in his basket. But all of a sudden, this tranquil scene is interrupted by Teddy's loud barking. Startled by the noise, you immediately lose the focus on your work. And as the deafening barking continues, you have no choice but to swivel around in your chair to attend to your dog. In your attempt to quickly calm him down (before the neighbours get upset), you give him a pat on the head and say "Ooh, Teddy - what's the matter, Sweetie, are you okay?" What you have just done is accidentally reinforced your dog's barking. And Teddy, the sweet Golden Retriever, is now well on his way to becoming a habitual "noise-generator", because he is learning that whining and barking is giving him what he wants: your attention and affection.

Now, let's take a step back and break down what has just happened between you and Teddy: He has displayed an undesirable behaviour - in this case, excessive barking. And even though you do NOT want to see this behaviour more often in the future, you *accidentally* have reinforced it. You have added something (*positive*) into the equation: the pat on the head and the verbal affection. Therefore, you are quite likely to see (or, in this case - to *hear*) this behaviour more frequently in the future. In this manner, you have successfully applied Positive Reinforcement - just in the wrong way!

Accidentally rewarding our dogs for mis-behaving is an extremely common mistake, and an understandable one: After all, we want them to feel better, and to comfort them like we would a child. And it is extremely difficult to stay stern and unyielding in the face of an adorable puppy - when all we want to do is to quickly make them feel good again. But as the example with Teddy shows, giving in to our instincts to comfort and nurture can work against us. Luckily it is easy to avoid these pitfalls of Positive Reinforcement, once we know what they are.

2) Negative Reinforcement

Now that we have explained Positive Reinforcement in more detail, let's proceed to its counterpart - Negative Reinforcement (*we are removing something from the equation – again, for a behaviour to be seen more often*).

Out of all the 4 areas of operant conditioning, Negative Reinforcement is the one area you want to use the least, or not at all. You will not have to: To raise and train perfect puppies, the other three sections of operant conditioning are more than sufficient. In my personal opinion, Negative Reinforcement should only be employed by experts in the field of advanced dog training. Such professionals know how to use the common tools of Negative Reinforcement in safe and fun,ways. Such tools include the prong- and the e-collar. In the hands of these trainers, such tools are not ever harmful for the dog. But they help the trainer to achieve amazing results within a short time frame. Negative Reinforcement is commonly used in advanced work with police- and military service dogs, personal protection dogs, and gun dogs.

Basically, Negative Reinforcement works like this: The trainer will remove a certain stimulus from the equation - respectively from the dog. This stimulus is often something irritating or unpleasant to the dog. An excellent example for using Negative Reinforcement is teaching recall. In this case, the trainer may activate the vibrate-function on the dog's e-collar. Which does not harm or hurt the dog - it is simply irritating to them. Now, whilst the vibrate-mode is activated, the trainer calls the dog. And the *moment* that dog starts coming towards them, they immediately switch off the e-collar. In doing so, the trainer essentially removes the unpleasant stimulus to have the desired behaviour (coming when called) happen more often in the future.

Now, this may be the first time you have ever heard about teaching a dog recall in such a way. But this method is highly effective - and can easily save a dog's life. Say, for example, your Beagle "Bella" habitually charges off whenever she has caught on to a scent. And unless you have her leashed all the time, she will, sooner or later, get herself into trouble: Even though Bella is a sweet Beagle who would never bite anyone, she could run unto a road and get hit by a car. In that case, Bella might get killed, and the people in the car might end up severely injured. Subsequently, you might find yourself at the wrong end of a lawsuit. If your dog is like Bella, and does not come to you *every single time you call them*, then you have two options: Option number one is to keep them leashed all the time. And there is nothing wrong with that. But if you do want to allow your dog the freedom to run off leash outside of your property, a perfect recall is a must. If your dog has not mastered this, then it is time to consider option number two: Seek the help of a reputable professional trainer. This trainer may very well use Negative Reinforcement in the ways we described. And after they have worked with your dog, your canine companion is free to run and roam in the great outdoors. But they will always be under your control. I can safely say that knowing this - knowing that your dog has mastered *perfect* recall under distractions - gives you a piece of mind that is worth gold.

Of course, using tools like the prong and the e-collar has been raising quite a few eyebrows in recent years, especially in the positive-only community: People tend to completely dismiss the use of Negative Reinforcement, claiming that it will not work. But that is simply not correct: Negative Reinforcement *does* work, especially when employed by an experienced trainer. Such a person can absolutely get a dog to repeat a certain behaviour over and over again. And they will not need many training sessions to do that.

E-collars and Prong Collars - a Word of Caution

Negative Reinforcement is highly effective. However, in my personal opinion, it should not be used by the average owner. As we said, for raising a regular companion dog, tools like the prong or the e-collar are not necessary. And most importantly, they can be easily abused by accident. This mostly happens when inexperienced owners want to utilise these tools as shortcuts to success in obedience training.

Let's take Mike and Cooper to illustrate what I mean by that. Mike is a middle-aged truck-driver who has always wanted a dog - preferably a Doberman. After moving in with his fiance, the time is finally right, and Mike decides to get a puppy: A sweet-tempered male called "Cooper". At first, everything goes well. But at six months of age, Cooper enters into his adolescence. And transforms from a mostly obedient puppy into a stubborn "teenager" who completely ignores Mike's commands.

Puzzled about this sudden change for the worse, Mike jumps online, and watches a few videos about the e-collar as training aid. He sees badly-behaved dogs transformed completely - in only one single training session. Mike is convinced that he has found the solution to his problems. He is sure that the e-collar will make Cooper revert to the sweet and obedient young dog he used to be.

What Mike fails to realise is: His problem with Cooper is not the dog's disobedient behaviour, but the lack of leaders in his life. Leadership that Mike has failed to provide for his young Doberman. And without that leadership in place, there is no (close and trusting) relationship. Which means the basis for an easy flow of communication between Mike and Cooper is broken.

Not realising this, Mike orders the shock-collar, puts it on Cooper and starts "working" with it: He runs through a basic sequence of commands, and "zaps" the dog pretty hard whenever he fails to obey. Believing a friend who told him that "Dobermans can handle a good amount of pressure", Mike cranks the intensity of the e-collar up to a fairly high level. Then, he starts delivering one painful electrical shock after the other to Cooper - whenever the dog fails to promptly obey his commands to "Sit", "Down", "Come" and "Heel". Cooper himself is so confused and literally shocked by the pain that he "fails" one command after the other. And before too long, the sensitive young Doberman has learned to associate the collar with inexplicable intense pain. He has no idea where this pain is even coming from. Why? Because he cannot make the connection: In the absence of a leash, Cooper is convinced that something must have bit him. He now feels fearful, anxious and stressed-out. And after a few rounds of electrical shocks, Cooper finally spins around and bites into the leg of the person standing closest to him - who happens to be Mike's fiance. "Oh my God, oh my God, I can't believe he did that!", Mike repeats over and over again, before he rushes over to Cooper, grabs him and throws him into his kennel. Then, he renders first aid to his fiance, who is bleeding and crying with pain. Whilst he rushes her to the hospital, Mike is shocked to his core. How could this have happened? This incident has convinced that Dobermans must be dangerous dogs after all. And that his only option might be to have his beloved dog put down.

Of course, the case of Mike and Cooper is a rather extreme example of what can happen when an e-collar is used completely wrongly. When it comes to the prong collar, however, things are not quite as dramatic: As there is a leash involved, the dog will understand that it is their owner who just corrected them. But if that owner does not know *precisely when* to give the correction, they can confuse the dog, and stress them out almost as much as with a wrongly used e-collar. Even worse: If the owner gets angry at their dogs, and keeps on yanking hard at the leash, they can actually injure the dog and leave them bleeding. This is especially the case when substandard prong collars are used: Collars with spikes that are not rounded off at the tips. Or collars that get rusty, and can cause serious infection if the prongs break the dog's skin.

In my personal opinion and experience, most dog owners simply do not have the knowledge and training that it takes to SAFELY use the prong or the e-collar. And by unwittingly abusing these highly effective tools, they undermine any trust their dog has ever had in them. They also destroy any leadership status they had established up to that point. But most importantly, such owners destroy the relationship. And as high level canine leaders, we do not ever want to break the relationship with our dogs - and their trust in us - by abusing Negative Reinforcement. Or by abusing any of the tools that are usually employed in it. So whilst it is important to understand Negative Reinforcement, you will most likely never utilise this area of operant conditioning. Which is why we are going to focus on the other 3 areas in this book. These are more than sufficient, and using them allows us to achieve incredible levels of success with our canine companions.

3) Positive Punishment

And now we are moving into the final two sections of operant conditioning - the ones revolving around "Punishment". Let's begin with Positive Punishment (*we are adding something into the equation to decrease the frequency of a behaviour*).

As a balanced behaviourist and trainer myself, I like to use every area of operant conditioning. But personally, I only use Negative Reinforcement in behaviour modification cases - and only if I am convinced that it will save the dog's life. However, when it comes to raising puppies, I exclusively focus on the other three areas of operant conditioning. In this way, I can take advantage of all the tools in my arsenal. And I can use them to raise and shape incredibly well-trained dogs: Confident, balanced companions who enjoy a wonderful, trusting relationship with their owner. However, I will not use any tools that would undermine that loving leadership, relationship and trust. And this is precisely why Positive Punishment requires great care and awareness.

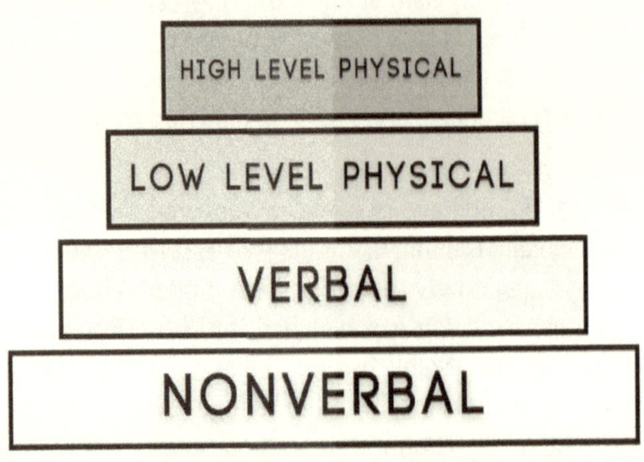

Diagram Number 6: The Hierarchy of Corrections

Positive Punishment contains 4 main levels of corrective measures, as illustrated above by diagram number 6. As high level canine leaders, our aim should be to stay on the lowest levels of the hierarchy of corrections: Ideally, we never have to leave the realms of nonverbal and verbal corrections.

Let's first discuss the large green rectangle making up the lowest level of our diagram - nonverbal corrections. These can be as subtle as a simple shift in posture and body language. And dogs are quite receptive to such minute changes: After all, this is their natural way of communicating. Mother dogs often use these body language-based cues to educate their puppies: If her babies get too boisterous, she will usually first assume an assertive stance, towering over them. And only if her babies disregard this warning will she move up the hierarchy of corrections - and use "verbal" corrections. This could mean she issues a low growl or a few sharp barks to keep her puppies in check.

Now, let's see how we as humans can tap into the enormous potential of nonverbal corrections. You remember Teddy from our previous example - the sweet but slightly unruly adolescent Golden Retriever? Now, let's assume you are sitting on the floor, playing tug-of-war with Teddy and his favourite rope-toy. Everything is going well, until Teddy gets a little bit too excited: He drops his tug-toy and starts painfully biting into your hands instead. This is quite a typical behaviour for a young dog. He might have simply gotten carried away - or he might be testing his limits.

If you have solid leadership in place with Teddy, this small transgression would require nothing more than a nonverbal correction: A slight change in posture and body language should be enough to make Teddy understand that you will not tolerate his nipping. To do this, you would get up from the floor, stand tall, chest out, shoulders back, assuming the pose of a confident leader (much like a mother dog would).

And it should not take your smart Golden Retriever long to "get the message" - after all, he will still remember such posturing from his own mother. So, if Teddy respects you as his leader, he should now understand and you'll notice the energy drop a level. This is it - mission accomplished! Once Teddy has stayed calm and displayed good manners for a bit, you can calmly resume your play session with him.

This example illustrates a little-known, but extremely important fact: If we have great leadership and relationship established with our dogs, this by itself will open our communication pathways to the maximum. Which is why we can almost silently communicate with our dogs – by using nothing but body language cues. If that does not work, we can always step up the hierarchy of corrections - and resort to a brief verbal correction. In this way, we are able to see the unruly behaviour happen less and less, with no physical correction whatsoever!

Taking a Step Back

But what if you find yourself having to climb higher on the hierarchy of corrections - right into the realm of physical corrections? Say for example you have an adult dog who is lunging at people, other dogs and maybe even cars. In such a case, an appropriate physical feedback to your dog might well be needed. And we will delve more into the topic of what such an appropriate

<u>correction</u> can look like in our next chapter. However, if you have a young puppy at home, you should not ever need to exceed the levels of nonverbal and verbal corrections.

But whatever age your dog might be, the root of whatever behavioural problem you might be dealing with is the same. And so is the "cure": If you feel the need to climb up the hierarchy of corrections above the first two levels, this indicates that your leadership and relationship is flawed. This is the problem. And the solution, the "miracle cure" to this problem, is quite simple. Make focusing on those aspects an absolute priority! Work on building up a solid foundation of good leadership and relationship. Of course, this is easier if your dog is still a puppy. But even if you have an adult dog who is displaying potentially dangerous behaviours, it is never too late to work on leadership: By all means, physically correct such behaviour. But at the same time, be aware that physical corrections without the foundation of leadership and relationship are merely a band-aid - not a fix.

How can you establish strong leadership and relationship with an adolescent or adult dog? I personally suggest putting them through my Boot Camp protocol - the 1 month strategy that I use with the vast majority of behaviour cases I work with. We have an online version you can check out at

<u>https://www.fenrirdogtraining.com/</u>.

Think of this as pressing the reset-button on your relationship with your dog. And once you have made progress in the bootcamp-process, you can then gradually climb back down on the hierarchy of corrections: Soon enough, you will no longer need to apply physical punitive measures: Verbal corrections will be quite enough to keep your dog under control at all times: Simply because you have become their respected calm, consistent and loving leader.

Again, if you have a puppy, things will be far easier. Just focus on establishing leadership. The easiest way to achieve this is by setting clear-cut rules, boundaries and expectations for your puppy. Then, all you have to do is enforce those rules, boundaries and expectations - calmly, consistently, and 100% of the time.

To summarize the problem of "having to" use strong punitive measures: *If your dog is ignoring your (first nonverbal- and then verbal) corrections, this is the tell-tale sign that your relationship needs work. This is always,*

always a warning sign that more work is needed. Of course, it can be tempting to simply reach for the highest level of correction in your toolbox - after all, you want to be efficient. But very few dogs need the highest level of correction, and it certainly is an overkill for puppies: If you take the time to build up leadership and relationship, all you will ever need may be the lowest levels of corrections. Staying low in the hierarchy of corrections requires more effort and skill than reaching for higher levels of correction. But it is absolutely worth it. And your dog will richly reward you for your patience and perseverance - with trust, obedience and impeccable behaviour.

Nonverbal and Verbal Corrections

On the level above nonverbal corrections, we have the verbal ones. These do not have to be entire words or sentences, like "No!", "Leave it!", "Teddy, drop it!" and so forth: Verbal corrections can also come as a variety of different sounds. For example, many owners (myself included) like to use a stern "Ah-ah-ah!" to discourage their dogs from unwanted behaviours such as nipping or chewing. Others use a different sound, like a shingling of keys, a clapping of hands or a short clicking sound. So, you can get creative with this, and use whatever works best for you. The purpose of these "verbal" corrections simply is to tell your dog that their current behaviour is unacceptable – and that you want to see it less and less often.

Personally, I use an "Ah-ah-ah!" whenever a verbal correction is indicated. For example, I might be working with a young dog who is nipping my hand. Usually, a decisive "Ah-ah-ah!" is enough to stop the unruly behaviour. Then, I redirect them to the desired behaviour, which could be to sit down, or to bite into their toy - instead of my hand. Once the dog is doing the desired action, I reinforce this with a small food reward or verbal praise. So, all I have to do is *correct, redirect and reinforce.*

Again, amongst their own kind, dogs use nonverbal and verbal corrections all the time. And very rarely do they even need to climb up higher on the hierarchy of corrections: All canines (our domesticated dogs included) communicate with each other through body language and sound *long* before they use physical corrections. Dogs are incredibly in tune with these kinds of corrections, simply because it is their natural way of communicating.

Physical Corrections

And yet, with some more extreme cases of canine behaviour, we might need to look into the realm of physical corrections. In our diagram number 6, we have two separate stages for this: low level, and high level physical corrections. The important thing to remember here is that "physical correction" does not mean we beat our dogs, punish them with electrical shocks, or strangle them with choke collars: For the average dog, moderate leash pressure or a gentle tap on the dog's leg are sufficient. (By the way, this mimics the way dogs physically correct each other - they nip the unruly pack member's neck or their legs).

For example, let's say you are out walking Bella, your beautiful Beagle, on a nice loose leash. Everything is fine, but suddenly, you are stopped dead in your tracks: Your canine companion has decided to stop and sniff the ground - instead of keeping up with you. Here, nonverbal corrections would be useless, as your dog is not even looking towards you. Gradually moving up the hierarchy of corrections, you attempt a verbal cue next, for example: "Bella, let's go!"

But Bella is too engrossed in that scent she is currently investigating to pay any attention to you. Okay - now is the time to use lead pressure to remind Bella: "Hey, you need to pay attention to me!" Once you have corrected Bella in this way, she finally lifts her nose off the ground and looks up to you. Now, you redirect her attention towards what you want her to do next - in this case, to assume the "Heel" position once again and continue walking by your side. You communicate this to Bella with a command like "Bella, Heel!". Once she starts walking to heel, you praise her. In doing so, you are following the basic sequence of dog training and behaviour modification: *correct, redirect, reinforce.*

Other cases of low level physical corrections include simple corrective tools, such as a slip lead or a Martingale collar. This might be all you will ever need, even for more boisterous dogs. And in my two decades of working with dogs, I rarely have come across a case that required more than a simple slip lead.

However, I am sometimes called in to assist with canine "death row" cases: Dogs who have killed another dog, bitten people or even mauled children. In these cases, I might have to move up to the highest level of the hierarchy of corrections. Not because I want to punish that dog for what they have done. But simply because I know that this dog will be put down - unless he changes his behaviour extremely quickly. Such cases do not give me the time to gradually make progress, using only my trusted slip lead: Here, behaviour modification must be achieved rapidly. And as being slow or uneffective would cost that dog's life, I usually will use a prong colour. (Other behaviourists, for example those based in the United States, might use e-collars in these situations. The specific tools we employ depends on our country's legislation, as shock-collars are illegal in some countries with them being in a grey area of the law here in the UK).

Working with such a death row case, I will utilise that prong collar to address and correct that dog's problematic behaviour as quickly as possible. For example, this could be an Akita that has severely bitten his owner - who then surrendered him to the local shelter. And now, this Akita is snarling, snapping and barking at everyone who comes near his kennel. This is a difficult and dangerous situation, because quite obviously, such a dog is prone to biting again. Or it could be an extremely reactive German Shepherd that lives in a constant state of fear and anxiety, and is highly reactive. Such a dog will not bite out of malice, but it easily could bite out of fear. Unfortunately, the results are the same: Someone gets bit, and the dog gets put down.

In these and similar cases, even one single session with a prong collar can significantly decrease those unwanted (or downright dangerous) behaviours. And after a few sessions, many of those dogs actually reveal their true nature: Once the mask of "bad" behaviour drops, we are faced with an amazingly friendly and affectionate dog. And by the way, this is the rule, not the exception! The vast majority of apparently severe cases can be resolved fairly quickly.

All these dogs needed was someone to finally step up, break the habit of the unwanted behaviour, and – most importantly – display some much-needed leadership. Most of these dogs never had any kind of leadership, rules or boundaries in their lives. But once they have experienced the presence of a calm, confident leader on the other end of their leash, they quite happily fall into the position of a follower. Because, as we have said before: *Dogs do not want to carry the burden of leadership.* They merely feel the need to take over because their owners fail to lead them. After all, every group, family or community needs a leader, no matter how small: Even if it is just you and your dog living in an apartment - one of you will have to lead. And if you fail to do so, your dog will. Simply because your dog sees no other way to stabilise your small family unit.

This is how people let their dogs down, and unfortunately, it happens all the time: Kind-hearted, well-meaning owners letting their dogs make their own decisions - and tolerating unwanted behaviours. Without meaning to do so, these owners put the burden of command squarely onto their dog's shoulders. And this not only puts a lot of stress on the dog, it also causes severe behavioural problems - right up to those death row cases that we just discussed.

Therefore, it is ultimately *leadership* that "saves the day" with these aggressive dogs who come with a bite history - and not the prong collar: High level physical corrections are not shortcuts to solving problems. But as balanced canine behaviourists, me (and my colleagues in other parts of the world) use certain equipment like the prong and the e-collar to establish leadership as quickly as possible.

Once leadership is in place, these severe aggression-cases are usually quite easy to rehabilitate. And often, my team can literally see "the weight of the world" is coming off of those dogs' shoulders: As soon as they realize that this human at the other end of the leash is taking charge, their entire demeanour changes. Their rigid posture relaxes, and they quite literally breathe a sigh of relief. But most importantly, the vast majority of these dogs will not have to be put down after all. Instead, they are now free to find a loving forever-home.

But how exactly do I implement Positive Punishment in these severe cases? As we said, there is much more to it than the high level physical correction in itself. Once the slip lead - or, in the most severe aggression-cases, the prong collar - is on the dog, I will start off with some basic directional changes: I will take the dog outside of the kennel and start walking him in a straight line to see how he is behaving on a lead. Then, I will introduce the first directional change. So, for example, I will give a brief verbal cue such as "Cooper, let's go!", then turn around and walk the other way. If Cooper ignores me and carries on walking, he will get a short pop on the prong. And the same applies if Cooper attempts to take his frustration out on me. He tries to bite me, but instead of succeeding, he receives more feedback from the prong.

The principle behind what I am doing is: Each time I give a gentle tug on the leash, I add something to the equation (the pop of the prong collar) in order to see a behaviour (Cooper's charging ahead or trying to bite me) less often. With dogs like Cooper, one session with the prong is usually enough to break the vicious cycle of the dog reacting aggressively, getting away with it, and repeating that same behaviour again and again.

But much as I would love to go into all the details of working with so-called dangerous dogs, it would by far exceed the scope of this book. Instead, let's now discuss why *you*, in all likelihood, will never have to use *any* high level physical corrections. Because I am convinced that – apart from these extreme cases -, we do not have to move up that hierarchy of corrections to the highest level. *"Getting it right the first time around"* is something I firmly believe in, and it is the basis of this book..

And what you are doing now is exactly that: You are taking the time to read this book on raising perfect puppies. In doing so, you are learning how to be a high-level canine leader: An expert owner who is going to build a wonderful relationship with their young dog. This loving, trusting relationship will then quite naturally open up the communication pathways between you and your dog. And because of this, you can start at the very bottom of that hierarchy of corrections, and you will hardly have to move up the levels at all: The better the leadership and relationship you have, the lower the level of corrections that you require. Therefore, if you want to see an unwanted behaviour less often, you need not go beyond nonverbal or verbal corrections. And you certainly will not need to use prong collars or e-collars for your dog.

Unfortunately, many owners do not take the time to educate themselves on raising perfect puppies. At least not before bringing a puppy into their lives. As a result, they run into trouble before too long: Instead of getting it right the first time around, they unwittingly create problematic behavioural patterns in their dogs. And usually, these problems get a bit out of hand once their puppy reaches adolescence. Quite understandably, these owners then seek the assistance of a local trainer. Which is a good idea, and by no means am I suggesting you should not do that. But unfortunately, there are trainers out there who take Positive Punishment too far. Because when it comes to the higher levels of that hierarchy of corrections, there is scope for abuse: Some trainers employ downright cruel methods of Positive Punishment, such as striking and punching the dog.

The purpose behind such drastic tactics is to see a certain behaviour less frequently – by adding something into the equation. However, inflicting pain on a dog in such ways simply is awful canine leadership. Going that route will invariably destroy any trust that dog has built up in their relationship. And as this trust is broken, the basis for their communication with the dog evaporates. From such a position, it is downright impossible to shape this dog into a perfect canine companion.

And you do not want to expose your dog to a trainer who will destroy their trust in people: Inhumane training methods can do severe damage to a dog's psyche, even if they bear no physical marks of abuse. I have seen this many times in my line of work, and it breaks my heart to hear these dogs (and their owners') tales of woe.

Therefore, please do apply caution and do not give your dog to just any trainer for a "Board & Train" program. If you are currently dealing with a badly behaved dog (adolescent or fully mature), do not rush into anything. Reading this book is a great start: It will give you a sufficient understanding of the principles of dog training to set you on the right track. Then, if you feel the need to hire a trainer, do your research first. Check what other people say about them. Talk to them in detail about their approach and methods, and visit their training facilities. Even if you like what the trainer tells you, I would still recommend you stay on the safe side: Instead of leaving your canine companion at their facility for "Board & Train", ask them to work with the both of you. ANY good trainer will be more than happy to do this. And it will help you to establish good leadership and a close, trusting relationship with your dog.

4) Negative Punishment

And now we have come to the fourth and last segment of operant conditioning, which is Negative Punishment (*we are removing something from the equation, aiming to decrease the frequency of a behaviour*).

Negative Punishment is a common tactic in dog training. And it is a perfect tool for raising and training puppies. Utilizing Negative Punishment is very straightforward: We simply remove things like praise, affection or attention from the dog. And this links back to what we just said about not needing *physical* corrections when it comes to raising puppies: Once you have established good leadership and an amazing relationship with your puppy, this can be all the correction they will ever need: In this ideal case, we do not even have to go into verbal corrections, and certainly not into physical ones. Because all we have to do is simply remove our attention. This alone will quickly lead to a decrease in the undesirable behaviour.

To illustrate this, let's go back to our friend Teddy, the boisterous young Golden Retriever. Teddy is an enthusiastic dog who loves people. Unfortunately, he also loves to jump up on people: Whenever someone gives him attention, he gets over-excited. All your efforts to correct Teddy's behaviour have failed. But you do not want to use harsh physical corrections either. The good news is: You do not have to! And this is exactly the beauty of Negative Punishment: It does not require any "punishment" in the traditional sense of the word. Instead, you simply take your attention away from the dog. So, if you wanted to apply Negative Punishment to reduce Teddy's ill-mannered jumping, you would do something like this:

To maximize your success, you start with controlling the variables. In this way, you avoid frustration, and you set yourself and Teddy up for success. As a first step, you leave the house for a good amount of time. Go and treat yourself to a nice cup of coffee, knowing that very soon, Teddy's pesky jumping-problem will be history. Then, after one or two hours, you come back home. By now, Teddy will be eagerly awaiting your return. As soon as you open the door, you see your Golden whirlwind rushing towards you. Evidently, he is getting ready to start jumping up. Now, your work begins: Instantly, you remove all attention from the dog. You physically turn away from Teddy, giving him neither touch, nor talk, nor eye contact. In this way, your smart Golden Retriever will very quickly learn that his boisterous behaviour is not getting him anything he wants, like your attention and affection).

At this point, just stay calm, keep on ignoring the dog, and go about your business. Hang up your coat, put your purse away, take off your shoes and so forth. And before too long, Teddy will calm down. Eventually, he will sit down and look at you - searching for clues as to what is going on. And THIS is success! This is the cue for you to now jump into the Positive Reinforcement zone - and shower Teddy with plenty of praise and fuss.

In this way, the unwanted behaviour of jumping up will soon decrease -

and the desired, polite behaviour of sitting and waiting calmly will increase. And not with just you: Teddy will soon apply this newly learned behaviour of sitting down and waiting to everyone else he meets. Of course, it might take him a few repetitions to catch on to this, but be patient – your efforts will soon pay off. In no time at all, you will have a wonderfully well-mannered dog who greets people like a dream.

Operant Conditioning Summed Up

As we have seen, some of the aspects of operant conditioning are not needed for raising and training perfect puppies. But by and large, all dog training uses operant conditioning: Even the most committed advocates of purely positive-only methods will dip into multiple areas of operant conditioning. Let me explain: Many positive-only trainers use verbal corrections. And in doing so, they are using Positive Punishment – they are adding something into the equation to see that behaviour happen less frequently. Another example is Negative Punishment, which means taking something away from the dog (again, to see a behaviour less frequently). What is being taken away could be attention, praise, or play.

One example of operant conditioning being used in a positive-only context is to discourage play-biting: Say for example you are sat down on the floor, playing with your puppy. And at some point, the puppy painfully bites into your fingers. A positive-only trainer might recommend you stand up and turn your back on the dog. Or to walk out of the room, effectively removing your attention from the puppy - and therefore using Negative Punishment.

Operant conditioning is a widely accepted learning theory for dogs. And it is used by the vast majority of dog trainers, canine behaviourists and expert owners. Of course, different styles of dog training will emphasize different aspects of the process. For example, trainers who follow the more dominance-based approach may emphasise positive Punishment. Positive-only trainers will favour Positive Reinforcement. What we are advocating here is a balanced approach that is fair to our dogs: We want to use the right tool at the right time, always taking into account our dog's age, breed, and personality. In doing so, we establish solid leadership. And this leadership solidifies our relationship with them - which ultimately leads to excellent communication. This is how we raise and train perfect puppies.

CHAPTER 2

Appropriate Reinforcement & Corrections

We have mentioned earlier how important it is to always set our dogs up to win: Rather than having to correct them all the time, we want to reward them for behaving well *most of the time*. But how exactly do we achieve that? The easiest method is to control the environment as far as possible. For example, we can train our puppies inside the house, having closed any doors or windows. In this way, we keep any outside noises at bay. Now, we have minimized the level of distractions. We have paved the way for our puppy to succeed. This could be something as simple as them performing "Down" for the first time ever. But to us, even such small successes are valuable. Because they allow us to now use Positive Reinforcement and reward this success. In this manner, we encourage them to lay down on command more often in the future.

My 90:10 rule of Reinforcement versus Corrections

And this is exactly what the my 90:10 rule of reinforcement versus corrections is all about: Ideally, we want to praise (in other words, reinforce) our dogs 90% of the time or more. And we only want to use corrections - ideally nonverbal or verbal -, 10% of the time or less.

So, what we are aiming for here is having our dogs succeed at least 90% of the time. Of course, we are not setting them up for failure *on purpose* for the remaining 10% of the time: But dogs do not succeed *all* of the time - they do make mistakes. After all, they are not computers or machines, and they are going to fail sometimes. Especially puppies and adolescents going through puberty are prone to misbehaving. We cannot avoid them making those mistakes, but we do need to correct them in these instances. At the same time, we want to avoid correcting our dogs more often than we reinforce them for behaving well. And this is exactly why the ratio of reinforcement versus corrections should be *at least* 90 to 10.

Let me put it this way: If you correct a dog, I would like to think that you have praised them at least 9 times before you have corrected them. If you are correcting them over and over again, you are clearly not creating enough opportunities to praise them! In this case, you need to take a step back and reevaluate your approach. Then, get proactive in seeking times when you can reinforce good behaviours. Violating the 90:10 rule can also mean that you are not controlling the variables effectively: In other words, you are not setting your dog up to succeed most of the time.

Now, a Positive-only person might claim that we can use reinforcement 100% of the time - using no correction at all. However, I personally do not believe this is possible, and I will explain why: To help our puppies grow into balanced, well-socialised and well-behaved dogs, we have to push them out of their comfort zone. Of course, we always make sure they are safe, and they are not pushed beyond what they can handle. But just like for us humans, growth and evolution occurs outside of the comfort zone.

Once our young puppy is fully vaccinated, the time has come for them to explore the world. At this point, we have the opportunity to increase their socialisation, and to demand higher levels of obedience and manners from them. And sometimes, they are going to fail and make mistakes which require corrections. This is completely normal - after all, they still are puppies!

But the trick is to try and control what we *can* control, such as the outer variables. For example, we can shield them from distractions whilst teaching them new commands, like "Heel" or "Down". We do this by first limiting our training sessions to the living room. Then, once our puppy has shown us a nice "Heel", or "Down" on several occasions, we take them outside into our backyard. There, we repeat the same commands, this time, with a little bit more distractions around: Perhaps you have a pen with chickens in your yard. And maybe there are dogs barking in the distance, people walking past your fence, or cars going by on the street. Whatever it may be - this outside training area will provide some distractions, but not enough to overwhelm your puppy. Because an overstimulated young dog is going to fail, and we want to avoid this at least 90% of the time.

And once your dog has nicely performed their "Heel", or "Down" in your backyard, praise them, give them food rewards, play with them - give them whatever they like best. In this way, you reinforce the desired behaviour. And also, you build a solid basis for all future training. Then, again, once your puppy performs well in the backyard, take them outside of your property. First onto a fairly quiet side street or field track . As soon as they have mastered their "Heel", or "Down" here, you take them to busier areas. There, you repeat the same principle again. You can continue with this step-by-step method until they perform well in almost any scenario: Eventually, your dog will give you a flawless "Heel", or "Down" in the most busy pedestrian zone. Every time they perform well, you reward them. In this way, they succeed most of the time, and you have succeeded in fulfilling the 90:10 rule of reinforcement versus corrections.

In this way, we can reduce mistakes to a minimum, and we set our puppies up for success. THEN we can shower them with all the praise we want them to have – and in doing so, we further reinforce those desirable behaviours. This is where puppy training (and dog training in general) becomes immensely gratifying and enjoyable for everyone involved. Because we can find new, fun ways of rewarding good behaviours, going out of our way to find times in which we can praise our dogs.

For example, let's say you are sitting on your couch, reading a book. Your dog is right there with you, being nice and quiet. Now, most owners would simply ignore the dog whilst they are behaving so well. However, as soon as they do something unruly (like start barking or chewing on a sofa cushion), they immediately jump in and correct them. But as high level canine leaders who aim to follow the 90:10 rule of reinforcement versus corrections, we do not ignore our dogs' good behaviour! Because in doing so, we would miss out on many valuable opportunities to praise our dogs - and to make that wonderful, well-mannered behaviour happen more and more often. Knowing this, we would not simply ignore our dog quietly lying next to us on that sofa. Instead, we might give them a small food reward or a cuddle. In this way, we are positively reinforcing that calm, quiet, well-mannered behaviour.

In Part 3, we have discussed the common mistakes people make in puppy training. And we have seen how easy it is to unwittingly reinforce negative behaviours: For example, in socializing our puppy, we can accidentally perpetuate our dog's fearful response to noisy trucks rumbling by. In such a situation, most owners make the mistake of trying to comfort their puppy.

To illustrate how this ties into the 90:10 rule, let's reiterate what we said about this common mistake in our last chapter:

"If our puppy is afraid of large lorries rumbling past them on the street, we naturally want to comfort them like we would a young child. So, we give them affection as soon as they flinch or jump. In this way, we unwittingly reinforce their fear. And in comforting them, we unwittingly tell them: "It's okay to be fearful, and if you react in this way, I'm going to give you what you want – fuss, praise, and maybe even a treat". Unfortunately, it is just as easy to accidentally positively punish a certain behaviour. A great example for this is us ignoring our dog whenever they are lying down in our office, being calm and well-mannered."

But now that we are aware of the 90/10 rule, we will not make these same mistakes again so easily. And if we do, we can quickly check ourselves and correct our approach. First of all, with the 90:10 rule in mind, we will set our dogs up to win, by carefully controlling the outer variables. So, in our efforts to socialize our puppies with lorries, we would first let them witness these large vehicles from afar. Then, we might take them to a layby, and let them experience the lorries there (which are either parked or moving very slowly). In this way, we can praise them for remaining calm in the face of lorries.

Equipped with this knowledge, we will find plenty of opportunities to praise our dogs. Then, we can use the 10% (or less) of recommended corrections to further strengthen our bond with them. Now, if you are a proponent of the positive-only approach, you might ask yourself: "How can punishing puppies help create a better bond?"

First of all, let me point out again that our corrections can be as benevolent as simply removing attention from the puppy. And secondly, not correcting them *at all* paves the way to them feeling insecure and confused. To avoid this, we need to let them know what we DO NOT want them to do.

In the line of my work I have seen too often what can happen when dogs do not know the rules: They get confused. A confused canine lives in fear and anxiety, and can easily develop behavioural problems. Therein lies the risk of a positive-only approach (of only ever reinforcing the good behaviours, and ignoring the bad ones): The confusion caused by this then breaks down relationship, trust and leadership. With the basis of successful training eroded in this way, anxiety and fear set in. This in turn causes an increase in unwanted behaviours, which can lead all the way up to fear-based aggression, resource guarding and other forms of potentially dangerous behaviours. And it is exactly this kind of behaviour that can make a sweet, lovely puppy grow up to become one of the death-row cases I have mentioned earlier.

Therefore, not only is it unfair to a dog to only ever reward them - it is downright dangerous. We need to clearly let our dogs know the Do's and Don'ts that we have set for them. And the best way to communicate those rules is to correct the dog as soon as they display an undesired behaviour. We do so in a loving, but calm and consistent way, like any good leader would. And this is precisely what our balanced training approach is all about. Its core principle is to let our dogs know: "Yes, this is what I DO want you to do!" But at the same time, we have the skills and the tools to let them know: "That is what I DON'T want you to do!"

In balanced dog training, we combine the two, and that is where people have amazing levels of success with their dogs. As balanced owners and trainers, we believe in calm, consistent leadership. And that leadership lets our dogs know what we *do* want from them, and also what we *do not* want from them. Which is quite similar to leadership in other areas of life, for example in business, and in our role as parents: For example, as a boss, I love letting my team know that they are doing a fantastic job. But if they are not meeting my expectations, I cannot simply ignore that: I have to give them clear feedback. Otherwise, I set my staff (and ultimately myself) up to fail. Because if I avoid providing the necessary feedback, my team becomes confused, then resentful. And eventually they will stop trusting me. Then, once the all-important basis of trust is missing, our relationship and communication falls apart. It goes without saying that this is a recipe for disaster for any business.

In a family setting, matters are fairly similar. I cannot ignore my children if they are drawing all over the kitchen wall, or if they are throwing their food onto the floor. Instead, I will let them know that this behaviour is not acceptable. They need to clearly understand that. Because if they do not, how can they trust and respect my leadership, my boundaries, rules and expectations? Only if they understand what I want from them - and what not -

, can they develop trust and confidence. In my own family, my children know exactly what my rules are. And therefore, they trust in me as a calm, consistent and loving leader. But if I only praised them for behaving well, I would be failing them as a father. Because soon enough, my kids will grow up to realize that the world out there is not only rainbows and butterflies: The society we live in has very clear rules and boundaries, and breaking them comes with a price. People who break the rules will get corrected. But as everyone knows the rules, people can make an informed choice whether or not they want to risk a transgression.

The 90:10 Rule Summed Up

As we have seen, clear, consistent feedback is crucial in family life, in business and in dog training. Without it, there is no balance, harmony, trust – or success. If children, employees, or puppies do not know what the rules are, how can they ever hope to win? If you have a puppy at home, and you sometimes reinforce a certain (good or bad) behaviour, and sometimes you ignore it, you are being inconsistent. Which makes your puppy confused and anxious: Your dog will feel that he cannot trust in you to always be his calm, consistent leader. Without this trust in your leadership, first your relationship and then your communication will break down.

So, everything really boils down to calm and consistent leadership - and about us almost being militant in our approach to corrections and reinforcement. If we have the self-discipline to be such high level leaders, then we will be rewarded with wonderful dogs: Perfect canine companions who are so well-behaved that we can praise them most of the time. And in this way, we fulfill the magical 90:10 rule of reinforcement versus corrections.

Appropriate Reinforcement

We have just spoken in detail about the 90:10 rule of reinforcement versus corrections. But what exactly ARE the best ways to reinforce - and correct - our dogs? There are many different ways to tell our dogs: "Good job - I like what you have just done!" And what is the best method for *your* dog really depends on them, their personality, and their individual preferences.

Most owners use food-rewards by default. For example, they tell their dog to sit down, and then reward them with a treat. But surprisingly many dogs are not food-driven. And trying to get a dog who is a picky eater motivated by food rewards can get frustrating fast. Luckily, there are other ways to reward good behaviour. Every dog is driven by *something*, and once we know exactly what that is, we are on the road to training success. So, whilst many dogs love food, some respond better to play. Others are motivated by both food and play, responding almost equally well to both stimuli. This is wonderful for training, as it gives us a wide array of options to choose from. Usually, these dogs have a sky-high play and prey drive. And they often belong to one of the common herding breeds (such as Collies, German and Belgian Shepherds) or hunting breeds (like Beagles, Pointers and Retrievers).

But what to do if your dog is equally disinterested in food and play? He might be a low-energy dog with a low prey drive, for example an English Bulldog or one of the Mastiff breeds. In this case, you have to rely on your dog's desire for your attention and affection: They might be quite happy to work for reinforcement in the form of verbal and physical praise. So, once they have sat down on command, you would praise, pet or hug them. In fact, quite a few dogs I know personally are more than happy to carry out commands for an enthusiastic "Good Boy!" or a simple ruffle behind the ear.

As dogs are motivated by different things, we should make every effort to find out what drives them most. This paves the way to amazing levels of training success. And then, of course, we use our dog's favourite reward as our most powerful training tool. Every time I begin working with any new dog, I first want to know what "makes them tick": What do they love the most? Is it food, praise, play, or attention? To find this out, I will usually put them through a series of simple tests: I will have a few toys with me in the training session, as well as some different kinds of food rewards. Then, I see how they respond to the toys, the food, and also to praise and attention. And here comes the important part: Once I know exactly what it is that drives this dog, I REMOVE it from them.

The Barrier of Entry

This does not mean I am being cruel, and I take away all the good things from this dog forever. But I will take them away *temporarily* – only to return them once the dog displays the desired behaviour. In other words, I put a barrier of entry in place. And behind this barrier, I put *everything that this dog sees as desirable*: The pieces of cooked chicken or hot dog, the tennis ball, the tug-toy, or whatever it may be.

Doing this goes hand in hand with the simple, but extremely important principle that everything that is good in our dog's lives comes through us. So, once I have put up that barrier of entry, I communicate to the dog: "I want calm and well-mannered behaviour from you. If you display that, I'll open the gate, and you can come in. Then, you can have access to everything you want: cuddles, praise, food, toys and even comfortable spots on the sofa."

All of these things can be utilized as Positive Reinforcement. But we do not want to bribe our dogs into compliance either. Therefore, a simple verbal praise ("Good boy!") or physical praise (a scuffle behind the ears) should be enough for the average job well done: And 9 times out of 10, that is all a dog gets from me personally. Because if all they have done is sit down on command, there is no need to go over the top with treats, praise and play. I highly recommend you *never* give your dog the things that he loves most, without him first showing you excellent performance. If he is not, then calmly correct, redirect, and reinforce.

And just as we always want to use the minimum amount of correction possible (nonverbal and verbal), the same applies to reinforcement. Therefore, we should save the high-value rewards (like tennis balls or sausages) for *exceptionally* wonderful behaviours: Such as our dogs coming back to us on call, even though they were in hot pursuit of a cat. Or maybe they jumped into the pool on command for the first time ever. Those are the times to get your high-value rewards out: Throw them their beloved tennis ball or hand out tasty pieces of cooked chicken.

But most of the time, we keep our dog's favourite rewards under lock and key. Because if we bring them into play every time our dogs do the simplest thing, these most cherished rewards lose their high value. Another thing to consider is that certain activities are rewards in themselves, and do not require us to pile more reinforcements on top of them. Let's say your dog knows that sitting and staying in front of the sofa gets him allowed on there. In this case, the act of allowing them up is enough of a reward. And the same can be said for walks: If your dog sits and stays nicely whilst you are getting ready, then you opening the door and taking them on that much-desired walk is enough. Or maybe your dog wants some affection. Again, displaying impeccable manners, they perform a nice "Sit & Stay" - and they wait until you are ready to turn your attention to them. In this case, giving them the fuss they were after is all the reinforcement called for by the situation: We do not always have to bombard our dogs with food and toys.

Appropriate Corrections

And when it comes to corrections, the same principles apply: There is no need to go over the top and use the strongest correction in our arsenal. Unless, of course, we are facing an emergency situation. But using physical corrections all the time is neither fair to the dog nor is it in line with our balanced approach to training. And it is not what a calm and consistent leader would do. We only ever want to use the minimum amount of correction applicable to the situation. And as we said before in the section about my 90:10 rule: If our dog is failing over and over again, we need to step up our game - and give them much more opportunity to succeed than to fail. In this way, we can praise far more often than we have to correct.

If you have put in the work upfront in terms of building up leadership, relationship and communication, you should be able to stay on the very bottom level of corrections. Which means that you only ever need nonverbal and verbal corrections. And yet, even the very bottom level of corrections has different degrees. The lowest form of correction can be something as simple as a click: A sound which the dog knows to mean that we disagree with their current behaviour.

For example, Sully, my yellow Labrador, knows that this click means "I don't like what you're doing - you need to look up to me for guidance and direction now. Because I'm about to tell you what I DO want you to do." If Sully is overstimulated or too distracted at that moment, he might ignore me. In this case, I need to step a level and use a verbal correction, like for example: "Ah-ah – Sully!" In this example, I am using Sully's name as a command. A command that is designed to get his attention, and to make him look up to me. Simply by saying his name, I am telling Sully: "I need you to snap out of what you are doing, and bring your attention back to me." Then, once my Labrador is looking up to me, I give him the next command, for example "Sit". And as soon as he sits down, I reward that desired behaviour. In doing so, I follow an extremely simple, and yet extremely effective, 3-step process that we have mentioned before. CORRECT - REDIRECT - REINFORCE.

In my day-to-day work as a canine behaviourist, I have talked to countless owners who felt they needed to apply strong corrections – even whilst their dogs were still quite young. More than anything, I want these owners to understand the connection between this perceived need for stronger corrections and leadership. Or rather, the absence thereof. What I need them to understand is that *their leadership is broken.*

Because if your dog trusts you and respects your leadership, you will have an excellent relationship with them. And having this amazing relationship means that your communication pathways are wide open. Therefore, you SHOULD need nothing more than a shift in body language, a click, or a verbal correction. Especially if your dog is still a puppy. When it comes to training puppies, I personally like to use a completely force-free approach. When done properly and with a strong focus on leadership, relationship and *then* communication, physical corrections of any kind are completely unnecessary.

If puppy owners are climbing up the hierarchy of correction quickly, they are not setting their dogs up for success anywhere near enough. They are not being calm and consistent canine leaders. And they lack the patience needed to let their dogs learn what they want them to do.

When it comes to appropriate corrections in puppy training, there is a rule of thumb: *The higher your level of leadership and relationship, the lower the level of correction needed.* This is absolutely crucial. I want to repeat this again, as it is so important to be fully understood: The higher your level of leadership and relationship, the lower the level of correction needed!

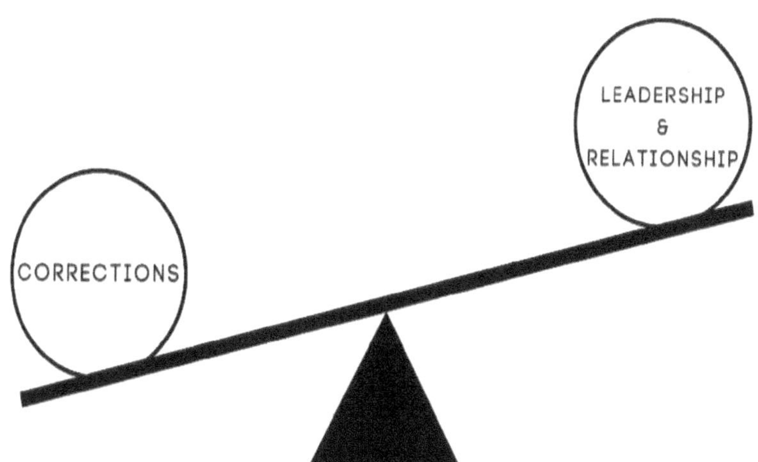

Diagram Number 7: The Correlation Between Corrections, Leadership, and Relationship

Which means that you can be very minimalistic. And removing your attention from your dog might be all that is needed. To illustrate this, let's say you are sitting on the floor with your puppy, happily engaged in play and cuddles. And at some point, your puppy starts to sink its little teeth into your fingers. This is normal puppy behaviour, and nothing to be worried about.

However, as a high-level canine leader, you do not tolerate puppy-biting. Not only because it can be quite painful, but also because it can escalate into more severe biting once your dog gets older. But most importantly, puppy-biting is a sign of your dog treating you like one of its siblings - instead of treating you like its mother, who is every puppy's respected leader: No mother dog would ever put up with being bit by her offspring.

The good news is that discouraging puppy-biting is quite easy. Especially if you already have established good leadership and relationship with your puppy. You can effectively stop them in their tracks by simply removing your attention: Get up and walk away. By doing so, you take away from your puppy what they want most: your attention and affection. This alone can be enough to discourage any further biting, at least for this particular play session. In this way, removing your attention can be an excellent correction.

This completely force-free type of corrections is highly effective - probably because it emulates the way canine mothers rein in their young. I highly recommend you watch some of the many videos available online about mother dogs correcting their puppies. More often than not, you will see "Mom" slightly shifting her body language. She may even growl or bark at an unruly puppy. In this way, she effectively (and quickly!) shuts down overly aggressive behaviour - without ever touching the puppy. Of course, being human, our ability to "play mother dog" is limited: Not even the most skilled trainer can beat "Mom" when it comes to peak-efficiency in puppy-correction. However, we can try our best to get as close as possible to the lofty standards set by mother nature!

Not needing to physically correct your puppy is wonderful in so many ways. It is great for your relationship, which will be built on respect and trust. And it means that you can save physical corrections for emergencies, or for potentially dangerous situations. Of course, you would physically intervene if you caught your puppy licking up coffee from the kitchen floor, for example. Not because you want to punish the puppy, but because you want to protect them (knowing that caffeine is toxic for dogs). Another example could be your dog suddenly lunging at cyclists whilst you are out on a walk. Again, you would use physical corrections to prevent accidents that could involve people getting injured or killed. And if your dog is aggressively attacking other dogs, physical intervention might prevent them and the other dog from harm.

Also, if you have a dog who suffers from severe separation anxiety, he might become destructive in the house. Some dogs rip apart sofas, others tear off entire door- or window frames. Even more severe cases might even smash through a window to get out of the house, cutting themselves in the process. If such an obviously unhealthy behaviour cannot be stopped by non-physical means then, again, physical intervention can be indicated.

3 Criteria for using Physical Intervention

And whilst I firmly believe that physical correction is hardly ever needed in young puppies, adolescent dogs can develop behaviours that make such intervention necessary. In fact, the examples that we have just discussed are typical for young dogs who are going through their puberty. Personally, I use the following 3 criteria for using physical intervention when it comes to training dogs.

Criteria Number 1 - The Dog is Causing Physical Harm to a Person or to Another Dog

This first Criteria is probably the most obvious one: It goes without saying that we need to prevent our dog from harming humans or other dogs. And not only to protect these humans and other dogs, but also to save our dog from becoming a potential death-row case. For these reasons, I do advocate using physical corrections in such instances. But even then, we still use the minimum amount required to achieve the desired outcome.

Criteria Number 2 – The Dog is Causing Physical Harm to Itself

Unfortunately, cases of dogs hurting themselves are not as rare as you might think. And these injuries usually occur in the context of severe separation anxiety. Such dogs can get into an extremely fearful state of mind when left alone, all the way up to a full-scale panic attack. In the midst of such a panic attack, a dog might cut itself whilst trying to get out of its crate. It might even try to get out of the house itself - for example by busting through a window or a garage door. Other dogs might scratch and claw at their crate (or at a door) so bad that their paw pads start bleeding. And some dogs injure their gums by chewing at their crate, or even by chewing themselves out of anxiety. Again, in my personal opinion, we have the obligation to protect our dogs from harming themselves in such ways. And if physical intervention is needed to prevent this, I believe that it does have a place here.

Criteria Number 3 – The Dog is Causing Significant Property Damage

Dogs damaging their owner's home by excessive chewing or scratching is a classical case for a canine behaviourist. And in the course of my career, I have been called into such cases quite often. Sometimes, desperate owners tell me that another trainer has tried to stop the destructive behaviour, but to no avail. – Which does not mean that the dog trainer was "bad" at his job. It simply means that such seriously damaging behaviour is outside the field of dog training: A trainer teaches a dog new things, whilst a behaviourist modifies negative behaviours.

For example, in my work as a behaviourist, I get asked to assist in cases where a dog has killed (or is trying to kill) other dogs. Or where the dog has a bite history with humans, or has caused thousands of pounds worth of property damage. In trying to help these dogs and their owners, I will enter those situations prepared to use physical intervention. But when it comes to training a puppy, a verbal correction should be all that is ever needed. Unless, of course, the young dog is displaying one of the behaviours we just discussed (which should not be the case, if you have been following the plan so far).

Appropriate Reinforcement & Corrections Summed Up

If you happen to raise a puppy as you are reading these words, always remember: Focusing on leadership will give you an amazing relationship with your puppy. And this will provide you wide open communication pathways - which in turn will enable your puppy to easily understand verbal corrections. And if they do not, then all you need to do is take a step back, and work some more on your leadership and relationship.

Dogs do that with each other all the time, using nothing more than a change in body language to communicate: If a dog wants to correct another dog's behaviour, it only needs to bare its teeth, or to issue a low grumble. Usually, the other dog will "get the message" quite quickly, and no physical correction is needed: Dogs communicate with each other, and correct each other, long before they *physically* correct each other. The reason this works so well is that dogs are very much in tune with one another, and they accept these types of corrections. However, they only accept the corrections of dogs whom they respect as their leaders: Dogs with whom they have a solid relationship, so that communication can flow freely both ways.

CHAPTER 3

Rules of Communication

No matter how old your puppy is, or what breed it belongs to - first and foremost, it is a dog. And all dogs absolutely thrive under the direction of a calm, consistent leader. Again, good, loving leadership leads to a wonderful, trusting relationship. And this in turn leads to perfect communication. On the following pages, we will speak about the easiest way to build this leadership, relationship and communication - with any dog, young or old. And no matter how long you have had them, or how badly they might behave. Never assume: "It's too late anyway for my dog - he's simply too old..." Or too energetic, too disobedient - whatever it may be. It is never too late, and even old dogs absolutely can learn "new tricks". When provided with high level leadership, even dogs in their golden years can learn how to be obedient, well-mannered and wonderful canine companions. And the simplest method to help them get there is establishing clear rules, boundaries and expectations. Once you are clear on those, you teach them to your dog. Remember: No matter their size, breed or age, dogs are extremely intelligent and adaptable. And they will quickly figure out that adhering to your rules, boundaries and expectations will get them what they want.

Rules – Boundaries – Expectations

What we said in our previous chapter about corrections will help us *reinforce* the rules, boundaries and expectations we have set up for our dog. But how exactly do we *teach* them those rules, boundaries and expectations? First of all, we (and everyone in our household) have to be clear on what they are. We have to ask ourselves questions like:

- Is the dog going to be allowed on the sofa?
- Can they sleep on the bed?
- What rooms in the house are off-limits for the dog?
- Can they lay next to the table whilst we eat - or do they have to stay in their place during mealtimes?
- How do we want them to react when the doorbell rings?
- Are they allowed to greet guests right away - or do they have to stay in their place until called?

Let's take the sofa, and let's say we have decided that our dog is allowed to jump on it. However, they first have to sit down, stay, and wait patiently. Then, once we give them the command "Jump up!", they can hop onto the sofa. If they do that, we allow them up. And if not, all we have to do is first give a verbal correction, then redirect them into a nice "Sit & Stay", and then reward them. In this case, allowing them up on the sofa is all the reward that is needed. Being high level canine leaders, we perform this entire process of correction, redirection and reward in a calm and consistent manner.[7]

If we persevere, repeating this over and over again, our dog will eventually learn: "Okay, if I do the negative behaviour, I am going to get a verbal correction. But if I do the desirable behaviour instead, I am going to get what I want!" Again, dogs are very smart, especially when it comes to figuring out how they can get what they are after. And it will not take your canine companion long to connect the dots: Very soon, they will not even go towards the undesirable behaviour of jumping up on the sofa uninvited, knowing that this will just get them sent down again. Instead, they will assume a nice "Sit & Stay" right away. And this is exactly how we use the tools of reinforcement, correction and redirection to get the fantastic dogs we want to have.

Do not Ask – Tell!

As humans, we generally prefer living in a democracy - no one really craves life under the dictatorship of another person. The desire for freedom runs very deep in human nature. But we must understand that dogs are different from us in that respect. We have said it before, and will say it again here, as this is so important for our dog's emotional well-being: Dogs absolutely need (and desire!) strong leadership. And any owners who shun being leaders, and who want their dogs to "enjoy their freedom, and just be dogs", are usually not aware of the damage they are doing to their canine companions.

When it comes to our relationship with our dogs, we have to do right by them – and to do that, we have to assume the leadership position. Therefore, the moment we bring a dog into our lives, we automatically have entered into a relationship where we are the authoritarian leaders of this dog. Essentially, a good relationship with our dogs is pretty much a dictatorship. Not in terms of us abusing our power, obviously, but definitely in terms of us *telling* our dogs what to do. Let me say this again: We TELL them what to do. We do not ASK them to do a certain thing - and then leave it up to them whether or not they feel like complying. If they respond in line with our command, they get positively reinforced, and if not, they get corrected, then redirected, and – again – reinforced as soon as they display the desired behaviour.

Of course, this does not mean that we are cruel to our dogs: A good canine leader does not have to beat his dog into compliance. Leadership is not established by means of cruelty, but by calm, consistent perseverance. Much of it is about the tone of our voice and our body language.

Once we have done all the hard work to establish good leadership and relationship, our communication pathways should be wide open. From this point forward, we need to do our best not to ruin this achievement with poor communication. For this reason, we should not enter into a discussion with our dogs. They are not humans, and they simply do not understand us trying to reason with them. So, let's assume that we have established basic obedience commands like our dog's, name, "Sit", "Stay", "Heel" and so forth. And this is all they need to hear from us: their name, the command, and then a marker. Let me give you an example of what such a basic sequence could sound like. I will take my own dog (Sully, the yellow Labrador) as an example. What I want Sully to do in this instance is quite simple: I want him to sit down. So, I use the following sequence to instruct him: "Sully – Sit – Good Boy!" As he knows his name, the command, ("Sit") and the marker ("Good Boy!"), this should be very straightforward. But note that I am not having a discussion with my dog!

If I were an inexperienced owner, out in public with my dog, you might hear me say something like this: "Sit - oh, you don't want to? Come on, sit down! Sully, please, could you sit down? SULLY! Come ON, sit down now! Sully – SIT!". At this point, I might turn to you, slightly embarrassed, and say "Oh well, he's not usually this stubborn!". Needless to say that such a discussion with our dog can get quite embarrassing in front of other people.

We have done all the hard work to establish good leadership, relationship and communication. From this point forward, we need to do our best not to give up our gains by failing on the communication front. The best way to avoid this is to issue our commands with firm determination. Remember: never ask - tell!

CHAPTER 4

DO's and DON'TS of Socialization

We have talked about the importance of socialization before, and we have seen how we can familiarize our puppies with new situations, sounds, animals and other things. In this section, we will cover a few Do's and Don'ts when it comes to socializing our puppies. Let's begin with the most common Don'ts:

DON'T Do too Much too Soon

Asking too much of their puppies too soon is a common mistake people make. And an understandable one: Of course, we are excited to show the world to our puppies, so that they can experience all the joys and wonders it has to offer.

But there is a time for everything, and puppies are delicate beings who should not be exposed to too many stimuli early on. Of course, and we have touched upon this before, growth does not occur inside the comfort zone - not for humans and not for dogs. But taking a young puppy into all kinds of unfamiliar, potentially scary, situations might overload their impressionable minds. And this can set you back for weeks in your training.

To illustrate an example of "too much too soon", let's go back to our previous socialisation-scenario where you take your puppy close to your neighbour's horse corral. But this time, you do not simply stop in front of the corral, but you pick your puppy up and carry them within 1 foot of a horse. And immediately, your puppy freaks out - they start, crying, squealing and squirming. trying to get away from the big scary animal. You then pet them and talk to them in a high-pitched voice, telling them "It's okay, Baby, it's just a nice horse, don't be scared!". But in trying to comfort them, you are accidentally reinforcing their negative response to that horse. So, the first mistake you will have made was exposing them to too much too soon. And the second one was to actually reward them for behaving fearfully.

DON'T Do too Little too Late

This one is directly opposed to the first mistake. And one good example of "too little too late" is the dog owner who believes that socialization is not necessary. Which does not mean that they are a bad dog owner: Usually, a person has very good reasons to believe that extensively socializing their puppy is not needed. For example, they could own a sweet and docile breed that is quite unlikely to ever become aggressive. Such as a Golden Retriever, a Goldendoodle, a Cocker Spaniel or an English Bulldog. Other reasons could include the person living very remotely, on a large cattle ranch, a farm or a house deep in the woodlands.

Dogs who live in such remote settings are always socialized to *something* (at least their human family members, the dogs and other animals living on the farm and probably some visitors). But they will not be familiar with the different scenarios, sights, sounds and scents of city life: Most working dogs on farms and ranches have never seen lots of people in one place, let alone cars, bikes and busses speeding past them. And neither have they been exposed to many different locations and situations.

Most of them are not even used to walking on a leash. And as long as such dogs remain in their familiar settings, they usually do fine. The problems start when these dogs finally do get taken outside of their established (and fairly small) comfort zone. This could be a vet visit or a road trip, for example. Then, their owners suddenly are faced with an extremely unruly or anxious canine, who is either pulling on their leash or trying to slip out of their collar.

Usually, these dogs are extremely insecure, which can lead to them barking at everything they see. By the time they finally get taken out in public, such unsocialized dogs are oftentimes well in their adolescence. And depending on their breed, they can be quite large and strong at this point. Let's face it: Any powerful dog who is not socialized and suddenly gets taken out in public is a potentially dangerous dog. Simply because it can (and will) behave in ways that could lead to trouble: Lunging at pedestrians, cyclists or other dogs – or even slipping out of its collar, running across the road and causing a car accident.

And whilst it is not impossible to socialize a slightly older dog, it is much harder: Once a dog's earlier socialisation stages are over, the windows of opportunity of socializing them with ease are closed. And in my work as a canine behaviourist, I get called in to help with countless cases of dogs who have become a danger to society – not because they are bad dogs, but because they have never been properly socialized.

But too little socialization done too late in a dog's life is not only potentially dangerous to other dogs and people: Such dogs can cause severe harm to themselves. Take breeds with an extremely delicate health such as the English Bulldog, for example: Generally sweet and mellow, these dogs are not likely to bite anyone. But if they are not socialized, and then get exposed to unfamiliar situations, they might work themselves into a panic. And a severely stressed English Bulldog might even suffer a heart attack and die. Such unfamiliar situations might include apparently quite harmless things, such as family visits, road trips or time spent in a boarding facility. Therefore, best to avoid doing "Too little too late".

Let's continue now with some of the DO's of socializing puppies, and we begin with the exact polarity of the DON'T "Too much too soon":

DO Start Slowly

Starting slowly is one of the most important things to remember when it comes to acquainting young puppies with the world. There is no hurry with this – socializing puppies is no race, And as long as you put in the time and effort required, day after day, you will be just fine. Be calm, consistent and persevering in familiarizing your dog with everything – but also, be patient: And do not worry about those windows of socialization closing at certain times: Just because the first socialization period ends around 12 weeks of age, this is not the end of the world. And it does not mean that you have "missed the boat" if your puppy is not perfectly socialized with everything by that time.

For example, if we go back to the case of the horses in your neighbour's corral: Your dog does not have to be comfortable with being nose to nose with a horse as soon as they are 12 weeks old: If they are comfortable watching a horse from, a few meters away, that is enough. Just continue your work, be perseverant, but not in a hurry.

Starting slowly can mean that you begin with standing 20 meters away from the horse corral, so that our puppy can see and smell the animals. Now, if they stay nice and calm, then we give them a reward. Then, we get a bit closer and repeat the same process – which is in essence rewarding the desirable behaviour of staying calm and relaxed in the face of those large animals. If at any point our puppy starts freaking out, no big deal: We simply move a step back, wait until we see that calm and quiet behaviour again, and reward our puppy for that.

If we proceed as suggested, then our puppy will have had TIME to observe from a distance. And they will have learned that they get rewarded for staying quiet. The same applies to other livestock, as well as busy roads, roadworks and so forth. Such a process of socialization to one single type of animal (or vehicle) can be stretched over weeks, or even months. Whatever it is that we are socializing our puppy to – we always start off easy, and then build up on that success, slowly but surely. If our dog freaks out, we never reinforce that, but instead, we totally ignore the behaviour, take a step back, and take it from there. And I promise you: If you give the process the time that it takes, you will be well on your way to having a well-socialized dog.

DO Keep it Up

Many owners do great when it comes to socializing their puppy: They take them on multiple walks per day, let them play with other friendly dogs, have lots of people pet them and so forth. This is awesome, and soon enough, their efforts will be rewarded by a well-balanced young dog whom they can take along wherever they go.

But sometimes, these owners stop at some point along the way, and for various reasons: Maybe they have moved to a more remote area, or they think that their work is done once the dog has reached a certain age. So, they stop taking them to town, or to other busy places. Instead, these owners now only walk their dogs locally, or they hardly take them outside of their property any more. This is a common mistake. But even the best-socialized property-, farm- or livestock guardian will still need ongoing socialization. Because no matter how big your house, garden or land is, it cannot provide your dog with the stimuli they need to stay well-socialized. Simply because your home and yard does not (usually!) have plenty of different scents, sights and sounds to offer. Such as lots of people, dogs, as well as trucks, cars, busses and bikes moving through.

And oftentimes, people write to me, asking me for help because their (once!) perfectly socialized young dog has developed serious aggression towards people. Once I inquire further into what exactly happened, I hear a similar story: As a puppy and adolescent, their dog was a dream to walk - friendly to everyone and quite unproblematic. But once the dog turned 12 or 18 months old, they stopped walking them all the time, trusting that their dog was mature enough to guard their house, farm, or livestock. They were convinced that no further work was needed. But as they stopped exposing the dog to various situations, he gradually lost his earlier confidence in dealing with the world "out there", and became reactive.

In such cases, I usually recommend going back several steps, and socializing the dog yet again to different environments: This additional socialization work has to be supplemented with a large dose of leadership, which will rebuild the close relationship that owner had with their dog before. In this way, we open the communication channels, and we can use all the tools in our arsenal to, once again, build up that dog's confidence: Simply by very consciously *leading* it in the various situations and locations that we now, again, expose it to. It is safe to say that socialization never stops, and we must not slack in our efforts to letting our dogs experience the fascinating world we live in.

DO Ask For Assistance

Asking other people for assistance in socializing your puppy is not something that is talked about often. And yet, enlisting the help of others can be invaluable when it comes to raising your pup to be a well-rounded, well-socialised adult. In our DON'TS section, we have mentioned the challenges of raising a puppy in a very remote setting, such as a house in the woods, a farm or ranch: Even if you want to socialise them, how do you go about it if the next town is many miles away? In these cases, you will need to get creative, and the help of others becomes especially important. Of course, nothing can replace you taking your dog to town or nearest settlement: Otherwise, they will not have the chance to experience road traffic, people milling about and all the different sounds and smells of those environments. And being familiar with this will come in handy when you have to take them to the vet, to the groomers, or to a boarding facility. But also, these experiences are necessary for your dog to be a perfect companion whom you can bring along on road trips and on visits to family.

However, no matter how remote you live - you do not have to wait until it is time for the next shopping trip to the nearby town: You can still work on your puppy's socialization every single day. Simply ask your neighbours, friends, family members or even visitors for assistance. For example, if your neighbour has a couple of very calm, friendly and balanced farm dogs, these "model dogs" can be priceless allies in your quest to socialize your puppy. (Of course, check with your vet first, and do not expose your puppy to any dogs that are not fully vaccinated, until it has received all its shots).

Also, when you have a young puppy, you want to invite plenty of different people over. Which will usually be quite easy to do, as the mere presence of a puppy will entice friends and family members to visit as often as possible.

However, if you do not have this opportunity, ask other people for assistance. This could be, again, neighbours, colleagues from work or even contractors and couriers. Usually, people will be more than happy to pet your puppy. And if they are hesitant, encourage them, saying how important it is for your dog to have positive experiences with as many people as possible. (In case of your mailman, he of all people should be an "easy target" for your socialization efforts: After all, his future well-being may well depend on whether or not your new guard dog likes him!)

So, I hope you find this short list of socialization DO's and DON'TS helpful. It may sound like socialization is a lot of work, and you may wonder why I am being so particular about it. But, again, from the standpoint of a canine behaviourist who gets messages about "problem dogs" every single day, I can assure you: You do not want to slack on the socialization front. And this applies to all dogs - not just to large, powerful breeds: Even the smallest dog can turn into a snarling, snapping nightmare if it is not raised properly. No one wants to walk a dog that aggressively lunges at every human or dog in reach. And you certainly would not want to live in a house that is ruled by a bloodthirsty Jack Russel Terrier, an out-of-control Yorkie, or a vicious Chihuahua.

But the *number one reason* why I am so insistent on the major importance of socialization is: Just like children, dogs need to see the world, and engage with life, in order to grow and evolve. Only through early exposure can these young beings grow into balanced, well-rounded adults: You cannot keep a child locked away inside a house all day, or never allow them to leave your farm. Both young humans and young dogs absolutely require lots of different experiences whilst growing up: They need to be exposed to plenty of different circumstances, situations and locations. And they need to interact with as many other people, and animals, as possible. Of course, this means that we (as parents and dog owners) have to push them outside of their comfort zone. Not too much at once, as we do not want to traumatize them. But we have to push them beyond their perceived limits regularly. And we have to do so in a calm, consistent and loving way - as any good parent, and any high level canine leader, would.

PART 5

TURBO TRAINING TOOLS FOR PUPPIES

And here we are, at the fifth and final part of our book on how to raise and train perfect puppies. In the previous four chapters, we have discussed operant conditioning, and the best ways to use it for training our dogs. Then, we have spoken about appropriate corrections and reinforcements for puppies and adult dogs. The last section of Part 4 revolved around fine-tuning our canine communication skills, and about the Do's and Don'ts of socialization.

In this fifth part, we will delve into the fascinating subject of training tools for puppies. We will start this section off with the question of why you have to be the gatekeeper to everything your dog wants (such as toys, treats, praise and more). Following on from that, we will speak about the various tools we can use to turbo-boost our training success. And we will close this last part of our book with a glimpse into the fascinating world of wolves in the wild. Because if we look behind the scenes of their daily routines, we can learn how to fulfill the deepest needs of our dogs. One of these lessons is the tremendous importance of exercise.

CHAPTER 1

THE Most Powerful Training Tool

Raising and training a puppy can be an immensely fulfilling experience: Hardly anyone is immune to the innocent charm, the trusting nature, and the open affection of puppies - not even seasoned trainers and behaviourists! And we should enjoy this process to the fullest. Young dogs grow up so quickly, and we want to make the most out of every single day with them.

Puppies can be annoying, and believe me when I say: I have seen, felt and suffered it all. I have stood around in my frost-covered garden in the middle of the night - freezing, and desperately wishing for my puppy to do their business. Of course, my dog did not share my sense of urgency - and took ten minutes to finally do the needful. Also, I have felt the frustration of coming home to my wooden staircase having been forever changed by my young Labrador's razor-sharp milk teeth. And let's not even speak about the countless times that I have cleaned up accidents of various kinds - or suffered under the onslaught of heart-breaking puppy-whines.

But no matter how taxing and troubling raising a puppy can be - there is light at the end of the tunnel. And after reading these next three chapters, you will literally have ALL the tools you need to raise a perfect puppy. Not only the physical tools such as toys, treats, collars and leashes - but also the real turbo-boosters for puppy training success. These turbo-boosters have everything to do with yourself, and with your ability to expertly lead your dog in every situation.

Because even the best physical tools are only ever means to an end. And that is ultimately what a tool is – it allows us to achieve a desired outcome easier and faster. *But these tools should never be used to replace the core principles of leadership, relationship and communication.* As your dog's trusted, calm, consistent and loving leader, YOU are the most important factor in their life. Not your fancy Flexi leash, your sparkly dog collar, the squeaky-toys in your closet, or the hot dog-treats in your pocket.

In fact, I personally know dog owners who have none of these physical tools to their disposal. All they have with them is a piece of string. Whenever they need to "leash" their dog, they use this extremely simple tool. And yet, these are some of the best-behaved dogs I have ever come across in my life. As this example shows, nothing beats your leadership, your relationship and your communication with your canine companion! If you have that in place, then all you may ever need in terms of tools is a simple piece of string...

Everything Good Comes Through You

And this ties in nicely to something you can do right away: An easy yet effective practise that will allow you to build up that all-important foundation of leadership, relationship and communication. In fact, I would highly suggest you make this practise a habit. This is something that you want to ingrain deeply in your way of interacting with your puppy. And by repeating it over and over again, day in and day out, it will soon become second nature to you. As it should, because this is not something you just do with your puppy: Every dog, no matter its age, breed or personality, should learn that ***everything good in their life comes through you***. In insisting on this, you effectively use everything your dog wants and values to enhance your leadership, relationship and communication! I know I have said this before, but I will say it again: YOU - along with your leadership, relationship and communication - are the best "training tool" on the planet.

Focus on building this foundation of leadership, relationship and communication. Make sure you are the owner and guardian of all the things and privileges your dog wants to have. Then, everything else will fall into place. Actually, this practise of making sure *everything good comes through you* is a tool in itself - and an extremely powerful one! In working with dogs for over two decades now, I have witnessed the tremendous potential of this simple habit: Time and again, I have seen "problem dogs' completely alter their behaviour for the better. Simply because, finally, someone in those dogs' lives stepped up and took the driver's seat - the leadership position. Because, in essence, this is what happens if you make yourself the gatekeeper for everything good in your dog's life: It makes you the leader. And in the canine mind, the leader owns everything: After a successful hunt, the wolf, or wild dog, who is in charge is also the first one to eat. When it comes to settling down, he (or she) lies down on the most comfortable sleeping spot. And even in terms of mating: In wolf packs, only the leaders get to procreate.

In other words: They own everything.

Everything Good Comes After "Sit & Stay"

By claiming everything that is good in your dog's life, you very strongly communicate to them that you are the boss. By "owning" all the things your dog needs to survive and thrive, you create a strong foundation. Because by making yourself the owner of your dog's food, water, toys, treats, cosy sleeping spots etc., you build up leadership, relationship and communication. By continuously insisting that all these desirable things are yours, you also *maintain* a steady level of leadership: Being the gatekeeper of everything your dog wants is something you want to practise throughout their entire lifetime. Amazing obedience and impeccable manners are mere side-effects of this. In fact, owning all desirable things in your dog's life is the fast-track to having an obedient and well-mannered dog: Doing this calmly and consistently builds, and maintains, the foundation for excellent behaviour.

This is also where the tremendous power of Sit & Stay comes into play. Let's say your puppy has learned that sitting down and waiting quietly is going to get them what they want. They have also learned to look up to you for guidance and direction. Again, everything good comes through you. Once your dog has experienced this over and over again, they will regard you as their loving leader. A leader who gives them everything they need. And rewarding your puppy for having performed a nice Sit & Stay is automatic: Simply give them access to something they would like to do, or to have. This can be hopping up on the sofa, going outside, eating their dinner or grabbing their favourite toy. You can use whatever verbal cue you like to release them from their Sit & Stay. Personally, I prefer the "Break" command to tell the dog: "Okay, now you can get up and do what you want!" You could also use "Hop up", if you want them to come up on the sofa - or "Eat" for digging into their dinner.

The simple habit of using the power of Sit & Stay in this way will put you lightyears ahead of the vast majority of dog owners: Whilst other people are pulling their hair, complaining about their puppy's terrible behaviour, you will have the best time ever raising and training your dog. Being the owner (and provider) of everything good in your dog's life - and using Sit & Stay as a barrier to accessing "everything good" is crucial. And it is one of the best tools in your arsenal. This alone will allow you to build an amazing relationship with your dog, based on loving leadership and trust. And it will go a long way to giving you that well-mannered, dream canine companion that you have always wanted.

I assure you, if you implement this in your daily interaction with your dog, you will not ever want to revert to your "old ways" again. And you do not even have to take my word for it: Try this for a few days, and see the difference for yourself! If there is only one single thing that you take away from this book, it should be this: **Always, always, always make sure that everything good in your dog's life comes through you!**

CHAPTER 2

Puppy Training Tools & Equipment

Now that we have seen how important it is that everything good comes through you, let's see what "everything good" could look like: Most of the tools we will discuss in this chapter are highly desirable items for your puppy: Either because they are edible, because they are something to play with, or because they are valuable to your dog in other ways.

Training tools come in many colours, shapes and sizes. And we can roughly divide them in 3 different categories:

1. Toys & Treats
2. Praise
3. Training Equipment (collars, leashes, harnesses)

Before we delve into each of these categories, it is worth noting that training tools are an example of "not one size fits all": Just like people, all dogs are different. Of course, you can use the principles and overarching theories presented in this book for any dog - these fundamentals are not subject to change. And they allow all the flexibility you need to apply them to YOUR puppy: Once you understand these principles and theories, you can easily adapt them to meet the needs, and preferences of your own dog.

Because just like us people, not all dogs enjoy the same foods, games and activities. Among human beings, we have the laid-back type who absolutely loves to chill out on the sofa and watch TV. Others live for the next opportunity to go bungee jumping or mountain climbing. Most people are somewhere between these extremes of "couch potato" and "adrenaline junkie". Dogs are not that different from people in this regard. And that is where breed, age and personality come into play. By and large, all dogs fall into one of the following 4 categories:

1. Food-driven dogs
2. Play-driven dogs
3. Dogs driven by neither food nor play
4. Dogs driven by both food AND play

Because dogs are motivated by different things, we have to be flexible, and adapt our training approach to our dog's personal preferences. If we are smart in utilizing those personal preferences as high value tools for training, we will be rewarded with the desired outcome: An obedient, well-balanced and well-mannered dog.

Finding YOUR Dog's Turbo Training Tool
1. Food-Driven Dogs (Winston, The English Bulldog)

As an example for a food-driven dog, we have an English Bulldog puppy named "Winston". At 4 months of age, Winston is curious about exploring the world - but at a nice and slow pace. Like other puppies his age, Winston likes to run and play, just not all that much. What he lives for, however, is food. Whenever his nose picks up on the scent of hotdog, he starts drooling with joyous anticipation. And whatever else is going on around him, nothing makes Winston as happy as receiving a piece of the desired sausage into his snubby snout. Quite evidently, Winston the Bulldog is a primarily food-driven dog. And in raising and training him, the hotdog is the strongest tool in his owner's arsenal.

2. Play-Driven Dogs (Laika, The Siberian Husky)

However, what to do if you have a picky eater at your hands? To answer that question, let's look at a dog who is driven primarily by their love for play: "Laika" is an adolescent Siberian Husky who seems utterly indifferent to food: At 7 months of age, Laika has yet to overcome her disinterest in food rewards. She is a picky eater at best: Apart from slowly eating her meals when she is hungry, she barely touches food for the rest of the day. Laika not only scoffs at conventional dog treats, but even at the most delicious pieces of sausage or fried chicken. However, there is something else that Laika would do anything for: True to her nature as a sled dog, Laika the Husky loves activity. Her favourite thing in life is to chase things. Anything from squirrels to cats, and even birds. Giving chase is what Laika loves more than anything, so "the chance to chase" would be the perfect high value reward for her. Not that I recommend anyone to ever send their dog after cats to reward them! But *prey drive* is essentially the same as *play drive*. And Laika will be more than happy to channel her immense desire for the hunt to toys - such as balls, kongs, frisbees or tug-toys. So whilst Winston the Bulldog is primarily food-driven, Laika's favourite training tool is play.

3. Dogs Driven By Neither Food Nor Play (Sammy, The Great Pyrenees)

Now, we will discuss the third category of dogs - canines who are equally disinterested by food and play. I would imagine that some of these cases can cause their owners veritable headaches: After all, most books, blogs or videos about dog-training tell us that we should use treats and toys for training our puppies. But how do you teach a dog who is utterly indifferent to both food *and* play? And indeed, dogs of this third category are the most challenging when it comes to training. Or so you might think. However, we must not forget to take these dogs' breed, age and unique personality into consideration. Breed plays a huge part in the category a dog fits into. For example, most Mastiffs and large livestock guardians are born with a far, far lower prey drive than Siberian Huskies and other sled dog breeds.

"Sammy", a 5 month old Great Pyrenees, is an excellent example for such a dog. Even at his young age, this beautiful, snow-white mountain dog is quite low in energy levels: Sammy is about as laid-back as Winston, the English Bulldog. But contrary to Winston, who would do anything for his beloved hotdogs, Sammy is not overly eager about snacks: The sight of a sausage leaves him relatively unfazed: If he feels up to it, he might show slight interest, and nibble at it. If presented with a dog toy, he might engage a little bit: Carrying his plush toy around the house, or even playing a few rounds of fetch with his owner. But after he has had enough, Sammy will gladly leave the task of tennis ball retrieval to his owner. At first glance, training a dog like Sammy seems hard work. After all, how do you motivate a dog who is not eager about *anything*? First of all, we have to realise that **every dog wants *something*.**

Let's say Sammy is your dog. And you have succeeded in what I personally like to call "getting it right the first time around": Being a calm, consistent canine leader, you have established firm leadership and a strong relationship with Sammy. From early puppyhood onwards, Sammy has learned to respect and trust you. Which means those all-important communication channels between the two of you are wide open.

This is fantastic! Because with this foundation of leadership, relationship and communication firmly in place, you are way ahead of the vast majority of dog owners. If I was standing in your living room right now, together with you and your young Great Pyrenees, I would first tell you that you have done a great job so far. Then, I would encourage you to ignore the wide-spread myth that food and play are the only ways to motivate and reward a dog. I would remind you that large livestock guardian breeds like the Great Pyrenees are naturally wary towards strangers. But at the same time, they are extremely sweet towards their owners. (And they will absolutely cherish your attention and affection - as long as you have that strong connection with them that you have with Sammy. If that is not in place, you have to work on it FIRST, before worrying about how to motivate your dog to perform commands!)

The close bond you have formed with your sweet, white Pyrenees puppy will absolutely work in your favour when it comes to teaching Sammy obedience and manners. It will also serve as a solid foundation for your socialization-work: Because Sammy trusts you and looks to you for guidance and direction, you will have no trouble at all training him. So, how can you effectively reward Sammy for a job well done? - Your trump card, your high value reward, is YOUR ATTENTION & AFFECTION. This is the turbo training tool to use for Sammy. As we said before, every dog wants something, and for dogs without a high food- or prey drive, this *something* is their owners attention and affection.

So, right there is your opportunity: Give Sammy all the affection, praise and fuss he wants - but only after he has performed a "job". This can be as simple as a nice Sit & Stay, or it can be an entire series of commands. A job well done can also mean Sammy has displayed impeccable manners (such as sitting and waiting patiently for your command before eating his dinner). Do not "waste your praise" by petting and hugging your puppy all the time. I know it is tempting, especially with a fluffy, cuddly breed like the Pyrenees. And sure enough, the Mastiff- and livestock guardian breeds produce some of the sweetest puppies on the planet! But resist the temptation. If you do, you are making your attention and affection the high value reward that it should be. So, whilst other dogs are driven by food or play, dogs like Sammy the Great Pyrenees are motivated by *attention and affection.*

4. Dogs Driven By Both Food AND Play

Now we are moving into the fourth and final type of dog. And here, we have the top-performers of the canine world: the Belgian Malinois, Dutch Shepherds, Border Collies, and Working Labradors. Having been selectively bred for high level performance in their respective field of expertise, these dogs are born with an extremely high prey drive. And usually, they are driven by both food, play and praise. If you have ever had the pleasure to watch a Malinois or Dutch Shepherd on a training field, you will have seen the handler using both food and toys as high value rewards. Usually, the person will have a small tug toy, or ball tucked into their jacket, and they will carry a pouch filled with dog treats. After the dog has performed well on a specific task, they will "pay" them by throwing the ball, or by getting the tug toy out for a brief play session. The food-rewards are mostly used to encourage good heel-work.

Coming from a dedicated working line, my yellow Labrador Sully falls into this fourth category. Like most Labradors, Sully is very much motivated by food. And he is even more interested in play: As soon as I get a tennis ball out, Sully's level of excitement goes through the roof. Whenever he sees a tennis ball in my hand, he transforms from being his fairly relaxed, happy-go-lucky, self to this intensely focused working dog. His entire world seems to narrow down into one single point - respectively, into one single ball. Sully is eager and willing to do anything to gain access to it: For him, the tennis ball is the King of all rewards - which makes it the highest value training tool in my arsenal.

But to maximize the use of this high value training tool, I have to restrict Sully's access to it. Because if I left tennis balls all over the floor - so he can play with them whenever he wants -, this tool would lose its effectiveness. To avoid this, I make sure that Sully NEVER has access to a tennis ball. Unless of course, I give him that access. Remember: <u>Everything good comes through you</u>! As tennis balls are Sully's favourite thing in the world, they are what I use to reward him for good work. For example, I might get a tennis ball out during a coffee break. As Sully comes to the office with me, he will be keenly aware of this - and he will want access to his favourite object on the planet. This is when we go outside and do some obedience work together. Restricting Sully's access to tennis balls is not only necessary to keep him sharp for my personal training sessions with him: It also helps me in rehabilitating other dogs.

Because quite often, I will bring my trusted Labrador along with me when I go out to work with client's dogs or rescue dogs at a shelter. As Sully is well-balanced and even-tempered, he is the perfect role model dog. In this capacity, he helps me in rehabilitating shy, aggressive or reactive dogs. So, whenever I want to introduce a distraction to the dog I am working with, I will ask somebody to get Sully out of his crate - along with a tennis ball. I can trust Sully to remain laser-focused on the person with the tennis ball, and to do any kind of obedience work I want him to do. Basically, Sully will be so focused on the tennis ball that he will completely ignore the dog I am working with. Which gives that dog the space to calm down - Sully's absorption with his tennis ball signals to the other dog: "You can relax, I'm not going to harm you."

Summary

In conclusion, we can safely say that EVERY dog has something they want more than anything else in the world. For some dogs, this is a tennis ball or a tug-toy. For others it is praise, attention and affection. And many dogs work best for food rewards. Whatever YOUR dog's favourite thing may be - you can absolutely use it as your top training tool.

Once you have found out what drives your dog, what "rings their bells" more than anything else, you have found the perfect turbo training tool, the ultimate trump card. All you have to do now is to FIRST remove access to that resource, and to THEN make your dog work for it. So, the principle is quite simple: *If the dog likes it, remove it, and make them work for it!* What "work" you ask of your dog depends on the situation. It also depends on your dog's age, breed, and their mastery of commands. For example, a 9 week old puppy might well deserve its favourite goodie for performing a nice Sit & Stay for the first time ever. A more advanced adolescent dog might have to wait for their reward until after they completed a 15-minutes heel walk. And a fully trained adult dog like my Sully would only gain access to his cherished tennis ball after a series of obedience drills - or after a particularly laudable deed: If Sully starts chasing a squirrel and breaks off his chase immediately when I call him, then, of course, he will get his favourite resource.

And this method of restricting your dog's access to their favourite resource is exactly how you keep your "turbo training tools" sharp at all times: If you stay true to this simple method, your dog will stay true to their devotion to their hotdog or tennis ball - even as they move into their golden years. This method is also how professional dog trainers reach extremely high levels of competition-obedience. Good examples for such experts are breeders and hunters who train gun dogs.

But the method of restricted access to a high value reward is also employed by trainers for police- and military working dogs - and with great success. The breeds primarily utilized by police and military are the Belgian Malinois and the Dutch Shepherd (a lesser-known breed very similar to the Malinois). Incidentally, these dogs are so eager to please that they will happily perform even without food-rewards or play. And this is the beauty of dogs that fall into this fourth category: Dogs with an extremely strong prey-drive: They practically come out of their mothers' womb equipped with an immensely keen working drive, and stellar levels of trainability. Therefore, their trainers will initially "pay" them with food-rewards and play. But soon enough, they will learn to perform extended, complex series of commands - for nothing more than a quick ruffle behind the ears and a "Good boy!" or "Good girl!"

Toys & Treats As Training Tools

When it comes to training puppies, people tend to rely on tools too much. Oftentimes, they think that tools are the quick-fix solution to the problem - with the "problem" usually being an ill-mannered, disobedient young dog. But more often than not, the cause for such challenges is hidden far below the surface: Unruly behaviour generally is a sign that your leadership, relationship and communication need work: Those three elements are the best tools in our arsenal (in combination with the principle "Everything good in your dog's life comes through you"). Let me say again what I mentioned earlier, because it illustrates exactly what I mean: I know dog trainers who use nothing more than a piece of string, and they have some of the best-behaved dogs you could imagine. These people never use treats, clickers, whistles or anything else - just a piece of string. If they need to leash their dog, they create a simple slip lead out of that string. A string that, by the way, would most likely not hold the dog IF they decided to lunge after something. But these dogs do not misbehave in such ways. Quite evidently, they enjoy an excellent relationship with their owner. They thrive under their owner's leadership, and they are looking to them for guidance and direction come what may.

As we said before, we have to take our dog's age, breed, and personality into account to select the best tools for them. No one knows your puppy better than you do. Therefore, you will already know what drives them most. Typically, they will either be driven by food, play, or affection. Use these tools sparingly - do not bombard your dog with affection, praise, treats and toys. Otherwise, they lose their effectiveness as tools! I know it is hard to resist the urge to give your puppy lots of cuddles and snuggles. And you do not have to do this: Simply insist that your dog does something *before* throwing them a ball, or leaning over to hug them. This can be as simple as doing a nice Sit, Coming to you on call - or just looking up to you attentively when you say their name. A small food reward can also be given to reward nice, calm behaviour: Such as lying down quietly in their place whilst you are working on your computer. By all means, enjoy giving them all these good things, but give them as rewards for good behaviour, for some kind of job well done. In this way, you make the process of training your puppy the most rewarding for yourself. Because as the weeks roll by, you will see your puppy growing into a perfect canine companion.

Toys

And now, let's look into a few common toys and treats you can use as high value rewards for your puppy. The first three on our list (balls, tugs and plush toys) are perfect for dogs with a high prey- and play drive. Fillable chew toys and interactive toys (also known as anti-boredom toys) are multi-purpose tools: You can use them for play, but also as treat dispensers. These toys are ideal for dogs who love to eat AND for dogs who prefer play. Almost all dog toys are available in various versions: There are toys specifically designed for puppies, for aggressive chewers, and for adult dogs of all sizes. Because obviously, puppies and very small dogs cannot carry massive toys around with them. And heavy chewers (like some Rottweilers,

Pitbulls and German Shepherds) will destroy a flimsy squeaky-toy in a matter of minutes. Therefore, again - take your dog's age, breed, and (chewing!) personality into consideration when shopping toys for them.

Ball Toys

Ball toys come in an amazing number of sizes and variations. You can buy virtually any kind of ball, either online, in supermarkets, vet clinics or pet shops. The range of ball toys includes the conventional tennis ball, the puzzle ball, fetch ball and the squeaky ball. For dogs who are fond of water retrieval, you can get floating ones. Tug balls with a string attached to them are ideal tools for tiring out athletic dogs: Obviously, you can use them to play tug. But the string also allows you to throw the ball much further than a plain ball toy. And contrary to the average round toy, tug balls do not roll away on sloped ground. If you live in hilly terrain, you will appreciate this extra benefit. I personally love ball toys, and enjoy playing with my Labrador Sully and his all-time favourite: The simple, good old tennis ball.

Tug Toys

Tugs are great fun for dogs, and I frequently use them in my work as canine behaviourist: Introducing a dog whose temperament I want to evaluate to a simple tug toy can be a quite telling experience. Because if a dog growls, or even lunges at me when I claim that toy from him, this obviously means there is some work to be done: This dog is displaying resource guarding - and many people who adopt adult dogs get bit that way. However, if a dog willingly gives up his tug-toy to me, this is usually a good indication that we have a safe dog on our hands.

But tug toys are not only useful tools to evaluate adult dogs: A good game of tug-of-war is also a fun way of engaging with our dogs of any age. If you have two dogs, they will quickly learn to play tug with each other. For this, any kind of rope-toy or tug-ring will do. Of course, as with the ball toys, there is an endless variety of tugs on the market. Some are more elaborate, for example the bungee tugger which consists of a ball with an attached string and handle. Or the sheepskin chaser toy, which provides a soft biting pillow and is ideal for introducing tug games to puppies. The jute pillow pull toy (and its many variations) is a popular choice among guard dog trainers for introducing puppies into bite-work: Its consistency is similar to that of the biting-sleeve and bite-suit the dog will be trained with later on.

Training Dummies

Technically speaking, training dummies are more training tools than toys. Unlike conventional toys, they are primarily used by professional trainers, experienced handlers, and hunters. But nevertheless, any dog with a high prey drive will love to engage with a dummy. Most of them have a valve to allow adjusting their weight and firmness. This makes the tool ideal not only for adult sporting dogs, but also for puppies and smaller dogs. Retrieval dummies designed for gun dogs are buoyant, which makes them ideal for any dog who loves the water. If you use the retrieval dummy with your companion dog, however, make sure you teach them to bring back various toys and other objects *first* - before throwing the dummy out into a lake. Otherwise, you might have to swim out there yourself to retrieve the tool!

Plush Toys

Soft plush toys are especially well-suited for puppies. They are designed to help young dogs to alleviate discomfort from teething, and they come in nearly endless variations: There are soft squeaky toys shaped like hotdogs, chickens or pigs. Other plush toys look like ice cream cones, oversized strawberries or pineapples. But plush toys are not only popular among puppies: Adult dogs love these light-weight toys as well, as they are quite comfortable to hold and carry around. However, soft plush toys are fairly delicate, so you would not give them to adult dogs who are aggressive chewers.

Fillable Chew Toys

One of my favourite types of dog toys is the fillable chew toy: This multi-purpose tool comes with one hole down the middle, or several holes down the sides. And these holes can be filled with treats, peanut butter or meat pate. Such toys are available in many different shapes, such as bones, balls, donuts or triangles. There are some for heavy chewers, for large, medium and small breeds, and for puppies. Myself, I like using the puppy-version of the fillable chew toy for crate training. To do that, I insert meat paste into the toy's cavity, then put the toy into the freezer. Such a frozen popsicle can keep puppies occupied for quite a while: Long enough, in any case, to bridge those first few minutes in the crate that often trigger separation anxiety.

Interactive Toys

Next, we have the realm of interactive toys. Also known as "anti-boredom toys", these are ideal to keep your puppy (and adult dog) occupied for a little while. All of these tools work in conjunction with food. Basically, you insert some kibble, or treats, into the toy. Then, you hand the toy over to your dog: Let them figure out how to extract the food from the contraption. Examples for such interactive toys are the popular Treat-Dispensing Ball Toy, the Hide-and-Slide Puzzle, the IQ Treat Ball or the Dog Activity Flip Board. Simpler versions of this kind of toy are the snuffle mat and the licking mat.

Training Equipment

And now that we have looked at a few types of dog toys, let's see what the market has to offer in terms of training equipment. As with toys, you would begin with the puppy-version of each of these (unless, of course, you have an older dog): Just like you would buy a fillable chew toy, plush toy or rope toy specifically designed for puppies, start with a puppy collar and a very light leash. And here are some of the most common training tools:

Clicker

Personally, I like clicker training, even though I do not use it myself. Simply because I prefer utilizing my voice for giving verbal reinforcement. And I dislike being dependent on a tool (the clicker itself) that I have to carry with me all the time. I think that clicker training is very useful to condition a dog. The clicking sound itself simply marks a positive behaviour, and with good timing, it is effective. Of course, you can also mark that positive behaviour verbally with a "Good boy!" or "Good girl!" - without ever needing a clicker. Nevertheless, clicker training can be really valuable for beginner owners: It allows them to work on their timing in a consistent manner.

Whistle training

Similar to clicker training, whistle training is using sound signals to communicate with your dog. Unlike the clicking sound, the whistle is not used as a reward, but as a command. To condition a puppy to the whistle, you would mark a certain behaviour with 1 pip, 2 pips, or 3 pips. For example, 1 pip could be the signal for "Sit", 2 pips for "Down", and 3 pips for "Come". Myself, I love whistle training, and I use it for my Labrador Sully. However, it lacks the simplicity of clicker training - which makes it not the best tool for inexperienced owners: To be effective, whistle training needs to be done with skill and finesse. If you want to use it, you have the choice between conventional whistles (which can be quite loud and shrill) and ultrasonic dog training whistles: Also known as "the silent whistle" or "Galton's whistle", these tools emit sound that dogs can hear loud and clear - but humans cannot.

Collars
Flat Collar

We are moving now into the wide range of dog collars. If you have a young puppy at home, use a soft, padded collar designed for young dogs. Personally, I am in favour of teaching puppies how to walk on a leash with a collar, rather than with a harness: Simply because it allows me to communicate more directly with the dog. Flat collars for puppies (and adult dogs) come in many variations. You can choose between collars made of textile, leather, artificial leather or a combination of these materials.

For puppies, you want a light-weight, comfortable collar that is easy to fit. And for dogs of any age, you need that collar to be safe: Clip collars may be quick and easy to fasten and unfasten. Their downside is that these clips can spring open in the most inopportune moments: For example, when your puppy lunges at another dog, a cat, a bicycle or even a car. This is extremely dangerous, because you think you have your dog secured - and the next thing you know is that your puppy darts out into the street! The best way to prevent this is to go for a collar with a metal buckle. These collars basically fasten like a belt, and they stay securely closed no matter what. Many accidents involving puppies and adult dogs are caused by material failure: Clip collars springing open, collars ripping or buckles breaking. Which is why we from Fenrir have designed various ranges of high-quality, extra-secure dog collars - along with harnesses, slip leads and other training leashes. If you are interested in checking out our products, go to https://fenrircanineleaders.com.

Choke Collar

As its name suggests, the choke collar constricts around the dog's neck once the leash tenses up - either by the dog pulling or by the handler giving a correction. Choke collars can be made of any kind of material (such as textile, leather or artificial leather). But more often than not, they consist of a simple chain with one O-ring on each end. Whilst choke collars can be used as corrective tools in dog training, they have one serious downside: There is no limit to their constricting effect around the dog's neck. The thing to bear in mind when using this tool is: Some dogs can get so agitated when seeing another dog, a cat, or perhaps a rabbit on a walk that they choke themselves until they pass out. Needless to say that this makes choke collars potentially dangerous for the dog's health: If a choke collar is used by an inexperienced owner, it can seriously harm, or even kill, the dog. Which is why I personally do not recommend these collars. There is, however, one safe version of the choke collar that I do recommend, and that is the Martingale collar.

Martingale Collar

Traditional choke collars used to be a popular training tool for many years. However, they have somewhat moved into the background, making room for more advanced tools like the Martingale collar. On the surface, the Martingale appears similar to the conventional choke collar: When the leash is tense, both collars tighten around the dog's neck. But the Martingale has an in-built safety-mechanism that prevents it from choking (and potentially harming) the dog: It can only tighten up to a certain extent. Martingale collars are brilliant tools: Not only for training, but also for keeping dogs safely secured on a leash. Take dogs with very slender heads, for example, such as Rough Collies, Lurchers, English Greyhounds and other sighthounds. Normal collars can easily slide off their neck if such dogs pull backwards on a walk. A Margingale will not - but it has to be well-adjusted to its wearer.

Prong Collar and E-Collar

We have discussed the use of the e-collar and the prong collar in Part 4 of our book (in the section about the 4 areas of operant conditioning). Again, I firmly believe that these tools should be left to professional trainers and experienced owners. In the hands of an inexperienced person, advanced training tools like the e-collar and the prong collar can do more harm than good.

Harnesses

Now, we come to the more traditional tools, such as harnesses and various types of leashes. Personally, I like using well-manufactured, secure and comfortable harnesses - especially for puppies. Whilst I do prefer a light, soft puppy collar to communicate with the puppy, the harness is my tool of choice when it comes to allowing them free reign. And I will give you an example of how I work with both of these tools: Let's say for example that I am outside with my 4 months old puppy. At this age, they have already learned the basics of walking on a leash.

Before I leave the house, I will put a comfortable, well-padded harness on the dog - along with their puppy collar. Then, I will clip my training leash onto the collar, and start off my walk with a bit of heel-work. The collar allows me to gently, but clearly communicate with the dog. For example, if I turn left and the dog keeps walking straight, the pressure on the collar tells them: "Oh, Will is going *that* way - I guess, I should do the same". Once I want to conclude the obedience-section of my walk, I clip my leash into the harness, and give the dog a "Break!" command. In this way, I tell them: "Heel-work is over - now you can go and explore a bit!" The harness allows for maximum comfort whilst the puppy is sniffing around, and maybe even slightly pulling. (In this scenario, I am not concerned about pulling. Because all I have to do to stop it, is to give the dog a "Heel" command.)

However, many people think that using a harness will help their dog to stop pulling - and this is simply not true. I do not know where this myth has come from, but conventional harnesses do *nothing* to make a dog stop pulling on the leash. On the contrary: Harnesses were originally designed to allow dogs *to pull more effectively*. A harness allows them to pull into their chest (where they are strongest) - as opposed to through their neck, where they are very weak. Professional trainers and expert dog handlers use harnesses for protection work as well as for tracking. Other handlers use them for weight pulling or sled work. And these people use the harness precisely because they want the dog to pull freely, without causing itself any discomfort.

But of course, there is nothing wrong with the average owner using a harness for walking their dog: A secure harness can be fantastic in terms of providing additional security: It prevents the dog from slipping out of the collar. In this regard, it is similar to the Martingale. So, if the harness is something you are comfortable using, go for it! Just be aware that this is not a tool designed to circumvent heel work. Do not use them as a band-aid on the problem of not having your dog heel-trained. Teach your dog how to walk on a nice loose leash, and you will be quite independent from harnesses and other tools.

Having said that, there are harnesses specifically designed to help reduce leash pulling. And our own Fenrir-harness has that function built into it. The way these training-harnesses work is they have a D-ring at the chest plate. So, when the dog pulls, they essentially pull themselves around to the side - instead of pulling straight ahead, which is where they want to go. In this way, the Fenrir-harness (and similar models with a D-ring attached to the dog's front) are anti-pull harnesses. And they can be useful to initially break a dog's habit of pulling full-force: Switching a dog that pulls so hard they risk injuring their trachea to a no-pull harness is a good idea: I fully support any measures taken for the sake of a dog's health and safety. But once the habit is broken, I would advise such a dog's owner to start with teaching the "Heel" command. Once their dog has learned how to walk on a loose leash on command, the harness can be gradually phased out and replaced with a flat collar.

Halti

Haltis are essentially head collars for dogs. They work on the same principle as halters for horses, mules, donkeys, llamas or alpacas: People use them to guide the animal from one place to the other, for example from the stable to the pasture. In the case of a large, strong animal like a horse or a mule, the only safe way to guide them is by controlling their head. Because where the head goes, the rest of the animal follows.

Owners of large and powerful dogs often gravitate to the halti - the canine version of the halter - for the same reasons: They feel the need of controlling the animal on the other end of their leash. These owners use the halti for the same purpose as an anti-pull harness: To prevent the dog from pulling on the leash, or from lunging at people and other dogs they encounter whilst out walking. And whilst I do not use haltis myself, I would encourage people to use them in the same way as anti-pull harnesses: In my opinion, they serve the same purpose of breaking the dog's habit of pulling. But at the same time, the dog's owner should start with teaching the basics of heel-work. In this way, they make themselves - and their dog - independent from the tool. Because most people find it easier to simply slip a collar on their dog than to apply headgear everytime they want to take them outside of the house. (If you want to get a halti for your dog, make sure it fits snugly to their head. Otherwise, the tool can rub at the dog's face and cause itching and irritation. And the last thing you want is to have your dog paw at their face, trying to get a badly fitted halti off of their head.)

Leashes

Let's now jump into the most common tool for training - and walking - dogs: the leash. Again, if you have a young puppy, especially of a smaller breed, you would choose a very light version. The ideal puppy-leash should have a secure, but ight-weight leash clip.

<u>Training Leashes</u>

When it comes to selecting a training leash for your dog, there are countless makes and models to choose from. What kind you get depends on your dog's age, their size, and the kind of training you want to do with them. Say for example you want to teach your young puppy how to walk on a lead. In this case, you would pick a simple, smooth leash made out of a light material, such as rope or nylon. For easy and safe handling, such a leash would be relatively short. It should be equipped with a handle at one end - and a safe clip on the other. If you want to enjoy the benefits of walking your dog hands-free, you would use a slightly longer leash (about double the lengths of the simple puppy-leash we just mentioned). This leash would be equipped with multiple D-rings, which allows you more scope in adjusting it. You can easily loop this leash around your torso, either vertically, or horizontally around your waist.

Perhaps you want a training leash that you can use inside an enclosed area (such your garden or backyard). Your plan is to sometimes drop the leash and let your dog run freely. And this option is great to have for teaching advanced Sit & Stay, Down & Stay etc. - especially in combination with recall. For this purpose, you would again pick the simplest model (no need for excessive D-rings in this case). One important safety-aspect for this: Pick a training leash *without* a handle at the end! Otherwise the dog can injure - and even break - a leg when stepping into the handle whilst running full speed. (The end of such a leash can be knotted up for easier handling.)

Another type of training leash is the field lead, also known as tracking lead or recall lead. For puppies, choosing light-weight versions with bungee-effects is ideal. These leads are usually made of rope, nylon. Some of them are made out of a polyester-mix. This has the advantage of the leash being smooth, comfortable to handle, non-abrasive to the skin, water-proof and easy to clean: An important factor for training in muddy terrains. Field leads come in various colours and measurements - for example, 5 meters, 10 or even 15 meters.

Extendable Leash

By far the most popular among the longer leashes on the market, the extendable leash can be used for walking and training dogs. The vast majority of owners like to use these retractable leashes with the comfortable handle for leisure: They enjoy the comfort of providing a maximum of freedom for their dog without having to juggle long field leashes - that invariably get tangled up around vegetation, or the dog's legs. Extendable leashes come in two versions (cord and tape), and in various lengths (3, 5 , 8, or even 10 meters). There is one model available for each size of dog: toy, small, medium, large, and giant.

Slip Lead

Simple and easy, the slip lead is perhaps the most "primitive" dog training tool on the planet. And the cheapest: You can even make your own one - all you need is a piece of cord. Create a loop, slip it over your dog's head, and use the string to lead them. This ties back to what I said before about those owners who use just this simplest of tools - and who have extremely well-behaved dogs. But as with every other modern training tool: The market has an immense spectrum of different makes and models of the slip lead to offer. Personally, I prefer the well-manufactured and safe Fenrir-version: Unlike conventional slip leads, this model comes with an adjustable metal-plate. This metal-plate is designed to allow for an accurate calibration of the leash: It basically allows the lead to only constrict to the position of the plate, and not further. In this way, the Fenrir lead is comparable to the Martingale collar: It allows for clear communication with the dog, but without putting the dog's health and safety at risk.

Unfortunately, most dog owners use conventional slip leads much as they would a choke collar: They think that putting one of these tools on their dog will reduce their pulling on the leash. And whilst this may be true to an extent, most dogs will pull anyway, damaging their throats in the process - all the way up to a collapse of the trachea. .Especially if people try to further discourage pulling by yanking at the leash, they risk serious damage to the dog's throat and cervical vertebra. For these reasons, I highly advise people to be proactive - and to teach their dogs how to properly walk on a loose leash. Just do the work upfront with your puppy, be patient, calm and consistent, and you will succeed: You will have a dog by your side who walks nicely to heel. Then, you will not need to use tools like the choke collar or the conventional slip lead as "quick fix solutions". And, quite frankly, these tools almost *never* really are quick fix solutions.

Personally, the (adjustable!) slip lead is my favourite training tool - both for puppies and for adult dogs. In my opinion, this is all one ever needs for the average dog. And if I was to use one single piece of equipment forever with any dog, it would just be my trusted adjustable slip lead. Initially, I would add in some treats to reward good behaviours. But then, I would very quickly move on to verbal praise, and a bit of physical praise (such as a pat on the back or a ruffle behind the ear). If you have good leadership, strong relationship and excellent communication, that is all you need in terms of training tools.

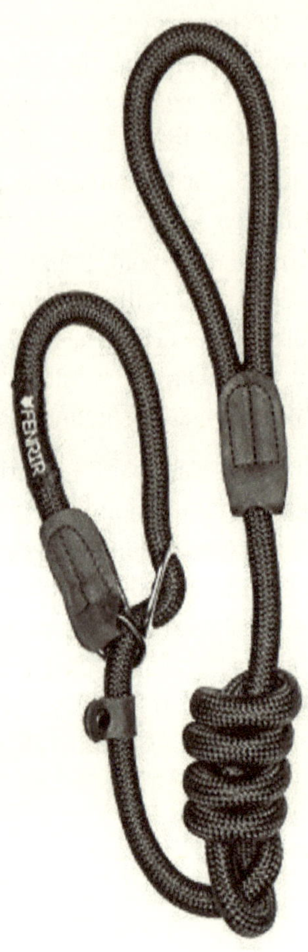

Other Dog Training Tools

There are a few other things which are not per se training tools - but you can use them to reward your dog for good behaviour. for example your dog's dinner, their walks, or their favourite spot on the sofa. All of these things are (usually!) quite high value rewards for a dog. And if you use them to "pay" your dog for a job well done - such as performing a series of commands, or sitting and waiting calmly and politely -, then they can absolutely be high value resources.

Again, always remember that these tools will lose their high value if you allow your dog access to them all of the time. Therefore, make them work for the privilege of jumping onto the sofa - or for being taken on a walk. And yes, even for eating their meal. Having to earn their food, their water, and everything that is good in their lives is natural for dogs: In the wild, packs of canines often migrate many miles in the pursuit of food and water. More often than not, they have to hunt before they get to eat. And on the hunt, they have to work together. If you have ever watched a hunting wolf pack, you have seen how well the wolves operate as a team: Much like a well-oiled machine, everyone knows what they are doing. And they all follow the guidance of their leader. In a domesticated dog's life, that leader is you. And even the most laid-back domesticated dogs expect to have to earn their meals. This is not "asking too much", on the contrary, it is very much in tune with their nature. For this reason: In demanding that your dog perform at least a few commands before getting to eat their meal, you are being a good canine leader.

Also, by asking your dog to work for their meals, their praise, their comfortable spots on your furniture and so forth, you reinforce the important principle that *everything good comes through you.* By making your canine companion understand that everything they want and value is given to them by you, you build and maintain strong leadership. (Just like the leader of a wolf pack builds and maintains his position by leading the group on their hunts, and to the waterhole.) Again, having everything needed for survival come through the group leader is natural for dogs. And with some practise, it will be natural for yourself as well. In this way, you will have laid the foundation for a relationship built on respect and trust. And ultimately, this will lead to an easy, effortless flow of communication between you and your dog.

Coming Full Circle

I would like to close this second chapter of Part 5 with restating what we said at the beginning: Training tools are amazing, but they are only ever means to an end - designed to make your job easier. They are fun to use, and there is nothing wrong with taking advantage of them. But I encourage you to maintain the bird's eye view when it comes to training tools: Ultimately, the ONLY tool you need in raising and training perfect puppies is yourself: As your dog's calm, consistent canine leader, YOU are the best tool at your disposal. Your leadership, your relationship and your clear communication with your dog are the best "weapons" in your arsenal. Focus on those, and then everything else will fall into place. Obedience, manners, and even social skills will come easy to your dog once these basics are in place. Be patient, be consistent, and you will succeed.

THEN, once these basics are firmly established, you can start to experiment with some of the other tools to take training even further. Whatever you do: Do not use gimmicky tools thinking that that will do the training for you - or replace the hard work that goes into leadership, relationship and communication. Once you have done the work to "get it right the first time round" with your puppy, as I like to say, you can play with different harnesses, leads, collars and toys. But always build upon the foundation of leadership, relationship and communication. Never use tools to try and replace that.

CHAPTER 3

Nature's Way of Exercising Dogs

In the previous two chapters, we have spoken about the immense importance of the principle *"everything good comes through you"*. On top of that, we have discussed some tools you can use to further enhance your training: Which is always based on good leadership, solid relationship and clear communication.

This third chapter of Part 5 ties into what we said in the previous section: Pouring praise, toys and treats over our puppies without discrimination means we are wasting our "ammunition" on firing blind shots into the air. Instead, we want to use our "ammo" to hit high-value targets. In this case, we want to use praise and play to reinforce SOME sort of good behaviour. But to start this chapter off, I want to stress the importance of exercise. Exercising your dog can - and often does - vastly improve their overall well-being and their good behaviour. More often than not, a well-exercised dog is better behaved in the house, more obedient and more social than a dog with lots of pent-up energy. Such a dog is essentially frustrated, and it will find outlets for its frustration: Such as excessive barking, playing rough, digging up your flower beds, chewing your shoes, or running through the house. This does not mean that you have a "bad dog" on your hands - you just have the canine equivalent of a bored and frustrated teenager in your house. Luckily, the solution is simple, and it can be summed up in one single word: EXERCISE. Or perhaps in seven words:

A Tired Dog is a Good Dog

In many ways, I use the phrase "A tired dog is a good dog" like a mantra - especially when I work with my clients. I want them to understand the vast importance of exercise for their canine companion's physical and mental well-being. Which in turn is an important factor in their own well-being. Because let's face it: If one single member of an otherwise happy household is unhappy, the entire household will suffer. And an unbalanced, frustrated dog is an unhappy dog. So, the path to happiness is blissfully short, but it is a path nevertheless. Meaning some activity is required on your part: You very literally have to walk the path. Together with your dog. As in: Take your dog for vigorous walks!

So, in this final chapter of our book, we will elaborate on the importance of exercise - in a healthy, balanced way that is natural for dogs. And in a way that includes the both of you: Exercise should never just consist of opening the back door and letting your dog out into the yard. Working out your dog should always be a team-effort - a team building exercise, if you will. Because first and foremost, it is natural for your dog to engage with their leader, both for training and for play. In this way, exercise solidifies leadership. Also, working out together with your dog is an amazing way to strengthen the bond between the two of you - in other words your relationship. We will also see why exercise and obedience training should come before affection and fuss. But before we jump into these fascinating topics, let us remind ourselves that exercising puppies requires care and consideration.

How Much Exercise is too Much?

Of course, how much exercise is optimal for your particular dog depends on many factors - such as breed, size, age and temperament. As your vet most likely will personally know your dog from their early puppyhood onwards, they are the person to ask when it comes to devising an exercise regimen for your canine companion. Over-exercising puppies and adolescent dogs can seriously damage the delicate growths plates in their joints. This in turn can lead to severe health problems later in the dog's life. Needless to say that surgeries for relieving orthopedic problems in dogs are quite expensive. For all these reasons, better to err on the side of caution. This does not mean making excuses, and not exercising your young dog enough. It only means: Check with your vet, and if you are uncertain, ask them to write down a detailed exercise schedule for your puppy. And then, once you know how much exercise they can handle at their respective age, make sure to give that to them!

Using Exercise to Boost Training Success

There is no doubt about it: Exercise is an immensely important part of raising and training perfect puppies. A tired dog is a good dog - well-behaved, and calm in the home. (Or, at least, *much more likely* to be well-behaved, and calm than a dog with lots of pent-up energy in its system.) But exercise also greatly facilitates obedience work, especially with puppies: Being so young and curious about everything, puppies get distracted quite easily. This can make obedience training far more difficult and frustrating than it needs to be. However, if your dog is tired out before you start your training session, they are less likely to get distracted. Then, you can keep them focused on the work at hand - and your training sessions will keep getting better and better.

The same principle applies to socialization: Before you take your puppy out to socialize them with new things, situations and places - play with them for a bit. Allow them to vent any excess energy - and *then* expose them to any new objects or situations you have planned for them on that particular day. Because socialization can cause young dogs to react in fearful ways, and we want to avoid that as much as possible: Whilst it is necessary to stretch them a little bit, taking them out of their comfort zone, on a regular basis, we do not want to overdo it: Rushing puppies on the socialization front is not going to get us anywhere. But if they are tired before we expose them to things they have not experienced before, they are far more likely to be relaxed - and to react well to the new stimulus: Because they are tired, they will be less distracted, fidgety and anxious. This means our socialization session will go much better than it would otherwise. And the same principle applies to manners: A tired dog is very likely to display the kind of behaviours we want. After a good, vigorous walk, run, or play session, our dog will most likely behave well in the house. As they are calm and quiet, you then have more opportunities to praise them for that behaviour: (Because they are tired, they will simply find a nice place to lie down, relax and sleep. Without us needing to pummel them with commands, or to correct them for running around, barking excessively, or being a general nuisance.)

Workout Schedule of Wolves in the Wild

In the wild, dogs and wolves have to migrate many miles to find food and water. Wolves and African wild dogs have been found to travel up to 30 miles a day. Even the medium-sized wild Dingoes traverse the unforgiving Australian Outback for around 25 miles every day. These are remarkable distances, and the canines travelling may not find food on every single outing, either. We can learn important lessons from mother nature in this regard, but we do not have to emulate her by depriving our dog of food, or by having them walk 30 miles every day before feeding them.

Many modern breeds are physiologically incapable of travelling such distances anyway: Large, bulky Mastiffs, lethargic English Bulldogs or short-legged Dachshunds are simply not built for covering lots of ground. Other breeds, like the German Shepherd, the working Labrador or the English Foxhound, could physically keep up with their wild cousins. But realistically, even the most capable of our domesticated dogs will never have the chance (or the need) to migrate for 25 to 30 miles per day.

So, what is the key take-away from this? There are several. First of all, ***the need to migrate is hard-wired into our dogs' brain***. Even if we own a tiny Chihuahua or a phlegmatic Pug, they are still dogs - and all dogs are born with the genetic predisposition to travel in the search for food. Even most of our modern dogs can trot for hours, and it is this kind of low-key trot that wild canines use to cover large distances. Of course, once the time has come to pounce, wolves and wild dogs start sprinting after their prey. They may not always catch their target, but they will try anyway. So, the second learning is there are essentially two major ways of exercise employed by canines in nature: *the trot*, and the *sprint* - the actual hunt. Ideally, we would emulate each of those for our dogs on a daily basis.

A Walk a Day Keeps Problems Away

Sometimes, people write to me saying: "I give my dog lots of exercise - but I cannot take him on walks." When I ask for reasons, the owner usually lists one, or more, of the following: "He doesn't like the collar / he can't walk on a leash / he pulls so hard I cannot handle him / he is so aggressive I'm afraid he'll bite someone." I completely understand that, for this person in this situation, all these are valid reasons to simply exercise their dog within the confines of their own property. However, personally, I would say: "Being able to take your dog on a walk is one of the most fundamental aspects of canine ownership. And if you cannot do this, you absolutely need to fix whatever the issue is."

Then, of course, whatever seems to be the issue on the surface (the aggression, the pulling and lunging - whatever it may be), is merely an indication of a much bigger problem. A problem that, more often than not, revolves around leadership, relationship and communication. Or, more to the point, around an ABSENCE of leadership, relationship and communication. But fortunately, the cure is simple: If you have a problem when walking your dog, walking your dog is the best way to solve this problem. Now, at this point, I can virtually see big question marks popping up in people's minds. 'Easy for him to say, he has no idea what I am dealing with here!' some of my readers may think.

As a matter of fact, I do have an idea, as I have personally rehabilitated many dogs who would not walk on a leash, who were lunging, pulling, or behaving like complete lunatics at the end of the leash. In all these cases, corrective tools help to manage the problem in the short term: An anti-pull harness, a halti, a slip lead and - with extremely dangerous dogs - a prong collar. But most importantly, the owner of such an ill-mannered dog will need to step up and LEAD. He or she will need to diligently work on building up good leadership, relationship and communication with their dog. Ironically enough, the act of walking their dog in itself is the best tool to establish such leadership - if done correctly.

Using the Leash to Build Leadership

In our previous chapter, we have discussed various training tools for puppies and adult dogs. And we have emphasised the necessity of teaching a dog to walk on a nice loose leash: Teaching good heel work not only makes walking your dog a much nicer experience, it also is an immensely useful way to establish leadership. Once this leadership is established, your daily walk with your dog will *maintain* it at a high level. Which will do wonders for the relationship and communication you have with your dog. If your dog is still a young puppy, you should have no problem teaching them to walk nicely to heel: Young dogs are eager to please, and will naturally look to you for guidance and direction. However, if you own a misbehaving adolescent or adult dog, you might need to get more assertive.

And you will have lots of opportunity to practise. Because with the help of your local dog expert, you should be able to reach the point where you can (safely!) walk your dog again. Once you are at that point, make walking them at least once a day your new routine. Even if you have a property that is the equivalent of 10 football fields, and all this space is available for your dog - they still need their daily walks with you, their calm, consistent canine leader. Nothing replaces the unique exercise in leadership and bonding that a walk provides.

But for the walk to unfold its tremendous potential, you have to go about it in a certain way. As a rule of thumb - always make sure you are leading the walk, and not your dog. Insist they stay in an approximate heel-position. Only allow them to venture to the end of the lead to sniff, explore and eliminate once you say so. This is absolutely crucial. In this way, you are using the leash to lead your dog. Whereas before, the dog has been using the leash to lead you!

How Wolves Walk their Canine Companions

What we just said about walking your dog directly relates to the way wolves and wild dogs work out every day: They migrate to find food and water, but not alone - their hunting trips are very much a team effort. For the hunt to be successful and for the pack to survive, all individuals must work together like a well-oiled machine. And operating that machine is the task of the leader: No matter the size of the pack, every wolf or dog has to follow the guidance of the pack leader. Firstly, they have to - literally - follow their leader to the location he or she deems best-suited for finding food. Then, whilst the pack is stalking the prey for the day, each wolf or dog has to watch for body language cues from the leader. If they fail to do so and blindly charge ahead, they can cause the hunt to fail - and the entire pack to go hungry. Were wolves and wild dogs undisciplined enough to disobey their leader, they would long since have become extinct. Long before humans ever had a chance to domesticate some of them, and develop the various dog breeds that we have today. In other words: We owe the sheer fact that we have dogs in our lives to the enormous self-discipline of their ancestors, the wolves.

Play Keeps Boredom at Bay

Whenever you are walking your dog, you are doing so much more than just walking your dog: There is a tremendous power in the ritual of the daily structured, disciplined walk. In insisting that our dog walks to heel, we are essentially imitating the proven best-practices of the high level canine leaders that came before us: the pack-leaders of wolves in the wild. If you doubt my words, just try to imagine a wolf pack setting out to look for food. Picture the younger and less experienced animals charging ahead, lunging at everything that moves - whilst completely ignoring their leader's signals to stop and remain behind him. How do you think such a group would fare in hunting? Not too well, to say the least!

So, the daily walk is the domesticated dog's equivalent of migrating in search of food. And PLAY emulates the hunt itself: The rush of chasing after something, and of sinking one's teeth into an animal that is about to be one's well-earned dinner. Like traveling, chasing the quarry down is usually a team effort. And wild canines practise their hunting skills from an early age onwards - by means of play: Play is one of the first activities very young puppies engage in. Our domesticated puppies behave in the very same way, and dogs seem to enjoy play until well into their golden years.

Myself, I absolutely love to play with my dogs, and playtimes have a firm place in the daily routines I have set up for them. I like to wrestle with my dogs, play tug with them, and reward them with a few rounds of fetch after an obedience training session. But I also enjoy watching them play with each other. Which is why I strongly believe in letting your dog play with others of its kind on a regular basis: Dogs are built differently from us humans, and our canine best friends should have the opportunity to wrestle, run and roam with other dogs. Of course, there are endless ways we can engage in play with them, and as we have seen, the variety of toys we can use is mind-boggling.

Daily Workout for Dogs = Heel Walk + Play (Run, Chase & Catch)

In balancing daily structured walks on a loose leash with vigorous runs and playtimes, we are using the formula for survival and success devised from mother nature:

Daily Workout for Wolves = Migrate + Hunt (Run, Chase, Catch & Kill)

Of course, our dogs have a different lifestyle than wolves in the wild. Which means, we need to adapt their exercise schedule. The basic principles, however, stay the same. For domesticated dogs, the disciplined daily "migration" will usually happen only with their leader But if other humans or dogs, are coming along, all the better: A "pack walk" is even more rewarding for our dog, as it emulates their natural way of travelling for food. Then, we have the other part of the equation (playtimes), consisting of running, chasing and catching. Most dogs are quite happy to simply run and chase - playing "catch" with a toy, other dogs, or their owners. As our dogs rely on us for their food, they do not need to hunt to survive. Therefore, the last but vital component of the "real-life" hunt (the actual act of biting down hard and killing the quarry) falls away. Unless, of course, a dog with a high prey drive happens to catch an unfortunate mouse or rabbit. Our domesticated dogs may occasionally run after cats or wildlife, but very rarely will a single dog be able to catch and kill game.

Balanced Exercise Makes Dogs Happy

Remember our catch-phrase from before: "A tired dog is a good dog"? A dog that has been worked out in the balanced, natural way we just described is a well-behaved and obedient dog. But the beauty of adequate exercise goes even beyond that: A tired dog is also a HAPPY dog. After all, we are borrowing our exercise formula *Heel Walk + Play (Run, Chase & Catch)* from mother nature herself. Exercising in this way is natural for our dog, and by being natural for them, it is designed to fulfill every aspect of their being. And a fulfilled dog is a happy dog. At the same time, a happy dog brings joy into our lives. We all have experienced dogs who misbehave in the home - either our own dogs or the pets of friends or family members. In all honesty, even for the most dog-loving person, this can be challenging. No one likes to be almost knocked over by a boisterous dog that launches themselves at everyone it sees. Or have their eardrums bombarded by an over-stimulated canine's deafening barking.

Kobe, the Cane Corso

And now, picture the contrary: Say for example your friends' Tom and Sally have invited you over for dinner. A few months ago, the couple got a new dog - a young Cane Corso called Kobe. You have not visited Tom and Sally for a while, so you have yet to meet Kobe, who will be almost 11 months old by then. You do not know quite what to expect, but you have heard that the Cane Corso is a powerful guardian breed - extremely territorial and suspicious of strangers. You know enough about dogs to be a bit concerned: After all, you are going to enter the territory of an adolescent guard dog. A dog who does not know you, and who would be more than capable of overpowering you. "Don't worry, you'll be fine, mate, just don't touch the dog - ignore him, and we'll take it from there." Tom's words of warning have not exactly put your mind at ease. But you decide to trust your friend's judgement.

So, when the time comes for your visit, you pull into Tom and Sally's driveway. As expected, you hear a deep and booming barking-sound coming from the house. As you step out of your car, lock it and approach the home, the front door opens. In the doorway, you see your friend Tom - flanked by a large, midnight black Cane Corso, who is staring at you intently. Your heart misses a beat as you realize the dog is not leashed. But Kobe the Cane Corso does not move. At least not until Tom steps forward, telling you to take a little walk with him and Kobe around the driveway. As you do, you are amazed by how well-trained Kobe is: He calmly walks to heel, eyes moving between his owner and yourself, the stranger. Evidently, Tom has trained his dog well. And after a short while, your friend releases Kobe from the "Heel" command so that he can approach you and greet you. Once first contact has been made, Tom invites you both back into the house. To your great surprise, Kobe immediately goes into his crate and lies down. He continues to watch you, but he does not bother you in any way. As you greet Tom's wife Sally, you comment on how well-behaved their young dog is: "Guys, that's just amazing", you say to them. "I've never seen a dog that doesn't jump, bark, and run around like crazy when people come to the house. What did you do to him? I mean, he's so calm, it's like he's on tranquilizers or something!"

Tom laughs and proudly reveals the secret to his dog training success: "It's funny, you know - everyone who comes to visit us says that about Kobe. But he wasn't always like that: As a puppy, he was as wild and crazy as any other dog. So, what we did was we set up an exercise- and training schedule for him. Every day, we give him all the exercise the vet says he can have. And we make sure he gets that FIRST - before we feed him, and before we leave the house. In this way, he is calm and content. Whenever we have people over, we do the same thing: First work out the dog, starting with a 30-minute heel walk. Then, we get back home and make sure he gets a good game of fetch with his favourite ball-toy. After he has cooled down a bit from play, we give him his evening meal. So, by the time you came over, Kobe already had his run off leash, he's had his game of fetch and his heel-walk. After that, we "paid" him for being such a good boy by feeding him his dinner. So by the time you pulled into the driveway, he was content and ready to settle down for the evening."

The experience you just had with Tom and Sally's Cane Corso Kobe is an amazing example for the power of exercise: Balanced exercise that consists of obedience work as well as vigorous activity. As Tom has just explained to you, tiring out your dog is incredibly important and useful. And it does not only help with obedience and manners - it also helps with anxiety. Because many dogs display destructive behaviours when left alone in the home. Usually, this is caused by separation anxiety, boredom, or a combination of the two. Exercising your dog well before leaving the house is the single best thing you can do to prevent destructive chewing. It is also a huge help for crate training: Crating a dog is much easier when they are tired. As Tom has told you: Because he had been tired out before you came to visit, Kobe was more than happy to calmly settle down in his crate: Tom's Cane Corso had been following the balanced workout schedule prescribed for canines by mother nature: Migrate & Hunt. Kobe had enjoyed "travelling" together with his leader (by doing a 30-minutes heel walk), he had successfully pursued and caught his "prey" (the ball-toy) - and he had gotten to eat the meal he just worked for (his dinner). Having had his primal needs met, Kobe was in a well-balanced state of mind. And by the time you came onto the scene, he was ready to rest in his comfortably padded crate.

The example of Tom and Kobe, his Cane Corso, shows the beauty of being a high-level canine leader. Like their "colleagues" in nature (the leaders of entrie packs of wolves or wild dogs), these leaders make sure the needs of their followers are met. They decide on when to set out on the search for prey. After the kill, they decide who eats first. And when the time comes to rest and relax, they get to "say" where this is done. If we follow the example of these natural canine leaders - the true professionals! -, we will succeed in raising and training perfect puppies. With hard work, patience and perseverance, we will raise the kind of canine companion everyone wants, but very few people get to have: A dog who is a dream to live with, and a joy to have around.

First LEAD, then LOVE

And this brings us to the very last section of our book on raising and training perfect puppies. The headline *First LEAD, then LOVE* relates to everything we have said so far. And it builds upon the fundamentals of leadership. Exercising our dogs is a key component of canine leadership, as we have seen: Four-legged canine leaders take their followers to waterholes, to promising hunting grounds - and back to their dens. They have a close relationship to their followers, and quite obviously, their communication works perfectly. (Otherwise, hunting success would remain elusive and, again, wolves would have gone extinct long ago.). But very rarely do canine leaders in the wild shower their followers with affection. They might return a subordinate wolf's licking of their snout with a few licks of their own. More often than not, approval is displayed silently, and in ways barely noticeable by us humans: With a look, a shift in posture, or a gentle nudge. Again, this is natural - the way things work in the wild, where survival is all but guaranteed.

Now, I am not saying that we should not give our dogs hugs and cuddles. In my own home, I absolutely love sharing cuddles with my dogs, and I am quite affectionate with them. However, in doing so, I apply the principle "first LEAD, then LOVE". Which basically ties back to what we said at the beginning of chapter 3: Instead of showering my dogs with love and affection, I insist on good performance first. Now, that does not mean they have to complete a one hour obedience drill first. It could be as simple as a dog calmly and politely waiting for me to finish whatever I am doing - even though the time for their mid-morning walk has arrived. (I keep my dogs on a very strict schedule: Routine is everything, especially for young puppies. And because they are "timed" so well, my dogs know when playtimes, walks, or meals are about to happen. Which is amazing, but being a good leader does not mean they get to make the decision for me: I still say when we go outside for a walk or a game of fetch.)

This entire fifth and final part of our book has been dedicated to training tools. And as we have seen, tools can come in many different shapes and sizes. Basically, everything our dog finds desirable can be used as a tool. This includes the most powerful training tool on the planet: YOU - your dogs calm, consistent canine leader. Like in nature, everything good comes to a dog (or wolf) through their leader.

This applies not only to the essentials of life, such as getting access to food and water - but also to other things that canines need to feel secure and fulfilled: Such as the security and protection offered by the presence of a strong leader - as well as the comfort and companionship offered by the other members of the group. What this means is that you are not imposing unnecessary restrictions on your dog by insisting that everything good comes through you. On the contrary, your canine companion is genetically hard-wired to expect that everything they need and want comes through you, their leader. This applies to all training tools available to boost your success in educating your puppy in manners, obedience and socialisation. The best way to use any training tool (such as a toy or treat or your affection) is to make yourself the gatekeeper to all the toys, treats and cuddles your dog could possibly want.

That is the meaning of "first lead, then love": Use your love, your affection and fuss, as the high value rewards, the "turbo tools", that they can be, and should be. Doing so gives you a dog who will readily look up to you for guidance and direction. First lead, then love, and you will effortlessly raise a perfect canine companion: A dog whom you can trust to follow your lead in every situation. A dog like Kobe, Tom's impeccably-behaved Cane Corso.